S0-CBU-175

AGRICULTURE IN THE U.S. FREE TRADE AGREEMENTS: TRADE WITH CURRENT AND PROSPECTIVE PARTNERS, IMPACT AND ISSUES

AGRICULTURE IN THE U.S. FREE TRADE AGREEMENTS: TRADE WITH CURRENT AND PROSPECTIVE PARTNERS, IMPACT AND ISSUES

REMY JURENAS

Nova Science Publishers, Inc.

New York

Copyright © 2008 by Nova Science Publishers, Inc.

All rights reserved. No part of this book may be reproduced, stored in a retrieval system or transmitted in any form or by any means: electronic, electrostatic, magnetic, tape, mechanical photocopying, recording or otherwise without the written permission of the Publisher.

For permission to use material from this book please contact us:
Telephone 631-231-7269; Fax 631-231-8175
Web Site: http://www.novapublishers.com

NOTICE TO THE READER

The Publisher has taken reasonable care in the preparation of this book, but makes no expressed or implied warranty of any kind and assumes no responsibility for any errors or omissions. No liability is assumed for incidental or consequential damages in connection with or arising out of information contained in this book. The Publisher shall not be liable for any special, consequential, or exemplary damages resulting, in whole or in part, from the readers' use of, or reliance upon, this material.

Independent verification should be sought for any data, advice or recommendations contained in this book. In addition, no responsibility is assumed by the publisher for any injury and/or damage to persons or property arising from any methods, products, instructions, ideas or otherwise contained in this publication.

This publication is designed to provide accurate and authoritative information with regard to the subject matter covered herein. It is sold with the clear understanding that the Publisher is not engaged in rendering legal or any other professional services. If legal or any other expert assistance is required, the services of a competent person should be sought. FROM A DECLARATION OF PARTICIPANTS JOINTLY ADOPTED BY A COMMITTEE OF THE AMERICAN BAR ASSOCIATION AND A COMMITTEE OF PUBLISHERS.

LIBRARY OF CONGRESS CATALOGING-IN-PUBLICATION DATA
Jurenas, Remy.
Agriculture in U.S. free trade agreements : trade with current and prospective partners, impact and issues / Remy Jurenas.
        p. ; cm
ISBN: 978-1-60456-418-1 (hardcover)
1. Produce trade—United States. 2 Free trade—United States. 3. Agriculture—Economic aspects—United States. I. Title.
HD9005.J87   2008
382'.410973—dc22   2008000889

Published by Nova Science Publishers, Inc. ✦ New York

CONTENTS

PREFACE[*]

Most of the U.S. agricultural export gains under FTAs have occurred with Canada and Mexico, the top two U.S. agricultural trading partners. Though U.S. sales to overseas markets were expected to increase anyway because of population growth and income gains, analyses suggest that the FTAs recently put into effect or concluded since 2004 could boost U.S. agricultural exports by an additional 2.0% to 2.7%. Large gains are also projected under the potential FTA with South Korea. Because of the reciprocity introduced into the agricultural trading relationship in those FTAs concluded with several developing countries that protect their farm sectors with high tariffs and restrictive quotas, U.S. exporters will benefit from increased sales. Net U.S. agricultural imports under these FTAs could be 1.4% higher than forecast.

The share of two-way U.S. agricultural trade (exports and imports) covered by FTAs has increased from 1% in 1985 (when the first FTA took effect) to 41% in 2006 (reflecting FTAs with 13 countries). Ranked in order, they are Canada, Mexico, Australia, Chile, Guatemala, Honduras, Israel, El Salvador, Singapore, Morocco, Nicaragua, Jordan, and Bahrain. If trade is included with nine other countries with which FTAs have been: approved but are not yet in effect (Costa Rica and Oman); concluded and awaiting consideration in the 110th Congress (Colombia, Panama, Peru and South Korea); recently took effect (Dominican Republic); and may be concluded (Thailand and Malaysia), another 9% of U.S. agricultural trade would be covered.

---

[*] Excerpted from CRS RL34134, dated August 1, 2007.

Trade in agricultural products frequently is one of the more difficult issues negotiators face in concluding free trade agreements (FTAs). While U.S. negotiators seek to eliminate barriers to U.S. agricultural export, they also face pressures to protect U.S. producers of import sensitive commodities (i.e., beef, dairy products, sugar, among others). FTA partner country negotiators face similar pressures. One U.S. objective is that FTAs be comprehensive (i.e., cover all products). For the more import-sensitive agricultural commodities, negotiators have agreed on long transition periods, or compromised to allow for indefinite protection of a few commodities. In addition, because of political sensitivities for the United States or its partners, negotiators excluded sugar in the Australia FTA, tobacco in the Jordan FTA, and rice in the Korea FTA.

Though food safety and animal/plant health matters technically are not part of FTAs, resolving outstanding disputes and reaching common understanding on the application of science-based rules to bilateral trade have directly affected the dynamics of concluding recent FTAs and/or the process of subsequent congressional consideration. One example has been the high U.S. priority to secure assurances that prospective FTA partners allow imports of U.S. beef in accordance with internationally recognized scientifically based rules.

Most of the U.S. agricultural export gains under FTAs have occurred with Canada and Mexico, the top two U.S. agricultural trading partners. Though U.S. sales to overseas markets were expected to increase anyway because of population growth and income gains, analyses suggest that the FTAs recently put into effect or concluded since 2004 could boost U.S. agricultural exports by an additional 2.0% to 2.7%. Large gains are also projected under the potential FTA with South Korea. Because of the reciprocity introduced into the agricultural trading relationship in those FTAs concluded with several developing countries that protect their farm sectors with high tariffs and restrictive quotas, U.S. exporters will benefit from increased sales. Net U.S. agricultural imports under these FTAs could be 1.4% higher than forecast.

The share of two-way U.S. agricultural trade (exports and imports) covered by FTAs has increased from 1% in 1985 (when the first FTA took effect) to 41% in 2006 (reflecting FTAs with 13 countries). Ranked in order, they are Canada, Mexico, Australia, Chile, Guatemala, Honduras, Israel, El Salvador, Singapore, Morocco, Nicaragua, Jordan, and Bahrain. If trade is included with nine other countries with which FTAs have been: approved but are not yet in effect (Costa Rica and Oman); concluded and awaiting consideration in the 110th Congress (Colombia, Panama, Peru and South Korea); recently took effect (Dominican Republic); and may be concluded (Thailand and Malaysia), another 9% of U.S. agricultural trade would be covered.

Chapter 1

RECENT DEVELOPMENTS

NEW TRADE FRAMEWORK

On May 10, 2007, House leadership (including that of the House Ways and Means Committee with jurisdiction over U.S. trade policy) and Bush Administration officials announced an agreement to include additional labor, environmental, and other provisions in free trade agreements (FTAs) awaiting congressional action. This step is expected to lead to congressional consideration of the FTAs concluded with Panama and Peru, possibly later this year. Whether this new trade framework advances consideration of the FTAs with Colombia and South Korea, which face strong congressional opposition because of labor union violence and auto issues, respectively, is uncertain. Though this framework is not expected to require changes to these four FTAs' agricultural provisions, domestic agricultural groups will be involved in the legislative process to point out either that they expect to benefit or not from these agreements.

SOUTH KOREA FTA

Minutes before trade promotion authority's (TPA) April 1, 2007, statutory deadline for the President to notify Congress of his intent to sign a trade agreement expired,[1] the United States and South Korea concluded an FTA. Formal signing of this FTA occurred on June 30,

2007. Agricultural issues received much high-level attention during the negotiations. Under the FTA, Korea would immediately grant duty-free status to more than half of current U.S. agricultural exports ($1.6 billion) and phase out tariffs and quotas for most other U.S. fruits, vegetables, grains, dairy products, meats, and food products in two, five, or 15 years. Korea succeeded in excluding rice from the agreement — a commodity that its policymakers view as vital to maintaining national identity and preserving economic activity in the countryside.

Though the FTA did not directly address the terms of access for U.S. beef into Korea's market because of concerns about past U.S. cases of bovine spongiform encephalopathy (BSE, or mad cow disease), some Members of Congress have signaled this trade agreement will not be considered or approved until Korea allows such beef to enter under scientifically based international rules in commercially significant quantities. South Korea's handling of U.S. beef shipments will be closely watched to gauge its willingness to implement a 2006 agreement and its President's pledge to expand upon its terms, and could affect the timing of when Congress votes on the proposed FTA.

MALAYSIA FTA

The deadline has passed for the United States to conclude an FTA with Malaysia that Congress could have considered under TPA rules that allow no amendments and only an up or down vote. However, both countries held a sixth formal negotiating session in mid-April 2007. Malaysia reportedly still seeks to exclude rice, but signaled it might agree to include tobacco in the FTA.

Chapter 2

BACKGROUND

U.S. farmers and ranchers, agribusiness firms, and food manufacturers view efforts to expand commodity and food exports as vital to improving farm income and business profitability. For this reason, many U.S. policymakers since the mid-1980s have viewed negotiating trade agreements as a way to create opportunities to increase agricultural sales overseas, primarily by seeking to lower and/or eliminate other countries' trade barriers (e.g., tariffs and quotas). To accomplish this, the United States has had to reciprocate by lowering similar forms of border protection on farm and food products imported from prospective trading partners. Because of the import sensitivity of some U.S. commodity sectors (e.g., beef, dairy, and sugar, among others) to the prospect of increased competition from foreign suppliers, the executive branch has had to take the concerns of producers of these commodities into account during negotiations, in order to secure congressional approval of concluded trade agreements.

The 1994 Uruguay Round Agreement on Agriculture negotiated under the structure of the multilateral institution that preceded the World Trade Organization (WTO) created substantial export opportunities for U.S. agriculture and agribusiness by partially lowering then-existing trade barriers worldwide. However, the U.S. FTAs that took effect with Canada in 1989 and with Mexico in 1994 (when both were combined into the North American Free Trade Agreement (NAFTA)) were more ambitious than the Uruguay Round in reducing barriers to bilateral agricultural trade. With these two trade agreements setting into motion a process that removed many, or will remove all, forms of border protection by the end of 10 or 15 year transition periods, respectively, Canada and Mexico became two of the fastest-growing markets for U.S. agricultural exports. During the period from the mid-1980s to 2001, the United States also entered into two other FTAs — with Israel and Jordan (table 1, top).

Table 1. Current U.S. Free Trade Agreements, by Date of Entry

Partner Country	Date Negotiations Began	Date Entered Into Force	Years in Effect
Negotiated under Earlier Trade Agreement Negotiating Authorities			
Israel	January 17, 1984	September 1, 1985	22
Canada	June 17, 1986	January 1, 1989	18
Mexico	June 12, 1991 [a]	January 1, 1994	13
Jordan	June 26, 2000	December 17, 2001	5
Negotiated and/or Concluded under Latest Trade Promotion Authority			
Singapore	December 4, 2000	January 1, 2004	3
Chile	December 6, 2000	January 1, 2004	3
Australia	March 17, 2003	January 1, 2005	2
Morocco	January 21, 2003	January 1, 2006	1
El Salvador (DR-CAFTA)	January 27, 2003	March 1, 2006	1
Honduras (DR-CAFTA)	January 27, 2003	April 1, 2006	1
Nicaragua (DR-CAFTA)	January 27, 2003	April 1, 2006	1
Guatemala (DR-CAFTA)	January 27, 2003	July 1, 2006	1
Bahrain	January 26, 2004	August 1, 2006	1
Dominican Republic (DR-CAFTA)	January 12, 2004	March 1, 2007	< 1

DR-CAFTA — Dominican Republic-Central American Free Trade Agreement
Sources: U.S. International Trade Commission, selected annual issues of the *Operation of the Trade Agreements Program* publication series; U.S. Trade Representative, *Annual Report of the President of the United States on the Trade Agreements Program, 1984-85*, February 1986, p. 97, and selected press releases accessed at [http://www.ustr.gov/Trade_ Agreements/Bilateral/Section_Index.html]; CRS Report RL31144, *The U.S.-Chile Free Trade Agreement: Economic and Trade Policy Issues*, by J. F. Hornbeck, September 10, 2003, Appendix 1; and CRS Report RL30652, *U.S.-Jordan Free Trade Agreement*, by Mary Jane Bolle, December 13, 2001, p. 1.
[a] Canada also participated in the initiation of NAFTA negotiations.

Since 2002, the Bush Administration has pursued a strategy that emphasizes negotiating trade agreements on three fronts — the multilateral, the regional, and the bilateral. This policy of "competitive trade liberalization" advocates using comprehensive bilateral FTAs as leverage to advance U.S. trade objectives in the multilateral WTO and regional (such as the failed hemispheric Free Trade Area of the Americas) trade negotiations, including those objectives laid out for agriculture (see next section).

Table 2. Status of Pending U.S. FTAs

	Date Negotiations Began	Status [a]
Prospective FTA Partners [b]		
Costa Rica (DR-CAFTA)	January 27, 2003	*Approved by United States:* [c,d] August 2, 2005
Oman	March 12, 2005	*Approved by United States:* [c,e] September 26, 2006
Peru	May 18, 2004	*Signed:* April 12, 2006
Colombia	May 18, 2004	*Signed:* November 22, 2006 Signed:
Panama	February 26, 2004	*Signed:* June 28, 2007
South Korea	June 5, 2006	*Signed:* June 30, 2007
Possible FTA Partners [f]		
Malaysia	June 12, 2006	Last negotiating round held in mid-April 2007
Thailand	June 28, 2004	Suspended by Thailand on February 24, 2006

DR-CAFTA — Dominican Republic-Central American Free Trade Agreement
Source: U.S. Trade Representative, selected press releases accessed at [http://www.ustr. gov/Trade_Agreements/Bilateral/Section_Index.html]; CRS Report RL32314, *U.S.-Thailand Free Trade Agreement Negotiations*, by Raymond J. Ahearn and Wayne M. Morrison, January 16, 2007, p. 1; CRS Report RL33445, *The Proposed U.S.-Malaysia Free Trade Agreement*, by Michael F. Martin, May 15, 2007, Appendix A.
[a.] See Key Steps before an FTA Can Take Effect (below) for an explanation of the terms used here to signify the different stages or steps that occur in the process of negotiating an FTA. b. FTAs that require actions that would lead to agreement taking effect, or await consideration by Congress and/or other country's legislature. c. Date that U.S. implementing bill was signed into law. d. Costa Rica's legislature is still considering DR-CAFTA, a process that may be completed by late 2007. e. Presidential proclamation to put FTA into effect has not yet been issued. f. FTA talks continue or are on hold.

Applying this strategy under trade promotion authority, the Bush Administration since mid-2002 initiated FTA negotiations with 23 countries, and concluded agreements with 14 of them. Of these, Congress has approved six FTAs with 10 countries. Agreements with eight countries have gone into effect (table 1, bottom). FTAs with two other countries (Costa Rica and Oman) have been approved by Congress but not yet implemented for various reasons. Four FTAs await congressional consideration (Peru, Colombia, Panama, and South Korea). Negotiations with Malaysia are continuing despite TPA's expiration, while talks with Thailand are suspended (table 2). See Key Steps before an FTA Can Take Effect (below) for an explanation of the terms used to signify steps from when the decision is made to negotiate through when an FTA is fully implemented.

This report looks at developments in U.S. agricultural trade with each current and prospective FTA partner, and the issues that came up during negotiations or that are still outstanding.

Key Steps before an FTA Can Take Effect Under Trade Promotion Authority (TPA)*	
The process followed in negotiating an FTA and seeking congressional approval involves several steps and can take a fair amount of time. With several terms (found throughout this paper) used to signify the major points in the process before a trade agreement can become law, the following generic schedule reflects the timetable laid out in trade promotion authority. This is to provide context for understanding the status of an FTA at any particular point in time.	
Decision to Negotiate	President must notify Congress of his intent to negotiate a trade agreement at least 90 days before talks actually begin.
Negotiations Begin	Negotiators from both sides sit down at their first meeting to exchange views and begin to prepare a negotiating agenda.
Negotiations Conclude	Negotiators make last minute compromises to clinch a deal, and make an announcement that they have concluded an FTA.
Signing of Agreement	Anytime after the talks conclude, President must notify Congress of his intent to sign an agreement at least 90 days before this occurs. Once signed, the President has discretion on when to submit the FTA to Congress for a vote.
Congressional Consideration	When the President submits an FTA to Congress, a 90-day timetable is set into motion for an up or down vote in the House and Senate on the bill to implement the agreement.

(Continued).

Approval	If both chambers pass the implementing bill and the President signs it into law, the FTA is approved. The FTA partner country's legislature, under its laws and procedures, must also formally approve the FTA.
Takes Effect or Enters into Force	Once both countries have approved the FTA and are satisfied that all outstanding issues pertinent to the FTA have been addressed, they decide on a date when the agreement's provisions will be implemented. Under U.S. law, the President issues a proclamation that amends U.S. tariff schedules to reflect the FTA's provisions, and specifies the date the agreement takes effect, or "enters into force."
* While TPA (Title XXI of P.L. 107-210) expired on July 1, 2007, the process laid out for considering trade agreements signed before that date still applies, irrespective of when the President decides to send an agreement to Congress for approval.	

Chapter 3

U.S. NEGOTIATING OBJECTIVES FOR AGRICULTURE IN FTAS

Since mid-2002, the Bush Administration's FTA negotiations have been guided by provisions spelled out in TPA authority in support of the overall agricultural negotiating objective: "to obtain competitive opportunities for U.S. agricultural commodities in foreign markets and to achieve fairer and more open conditions of trade in bulk, specialty crop, and value-added commodities."[2] Other stated U.S. objectives pertinent to negotiating bilateral FTAs are:

- to 'seek to' eliminate 'on the broadest possible basis' tariffs and other charges on agricultural trade;
- to 'seek to' eliminate non-tariff barriers to U.S. exports, including licensing barriers on agricultural products, restrictive administration of tariff-rate quotas, unjustified trade restrictions that affect new U.S. technologies (i.e., biotechnology), and other trade restrictive measures that U.S. exporters identify;
- to provide adequate transition periods and relief mechanisms for the U.S. agricultural sector to adjust to increased imports of sensitive products;
- to seek to eliminate partner government practices that adversely affect U.S. exports of perishable or cyclical agricultural products;

- to eliminate any unjustified sanitary and phytosanitary (SPS) restrictions imposed by the prospective partner and seek its affirmation of its WTO commitments on SPS measures; and
- to develop a mechanism with each partner to support the U.S. objective to eliminate all agricultural export subsidies in the WTO negotiations.[3]

In the FTA negotiations initiated by the Bush Administration, U.S. officials frequently have affirmed their position that no product or sector should be excluded, particularly when partner negotiators (in jockeying for leverage) seek to exclude their sensitive agricultural commodities from coverage in the final agreement. Also, U.S. officials repeatedly have made clear that the issue of U.S. farm support or subsidies, which some countries have sought to place on the FTA negotiating table, will only be addressed in the WTO multilateral negotiations.

Chapter 4

KEY AGRICULTURAL ISSUES IN FTAS

FTAs negotiated by the United States are generally comprehensive in scope. In addition to addressing market access for agricultural and food products, they cover trade in all other goods (including textiles and apparel), improved market access commitments for services and government procurement, protections for investment and intellectual property rights; and include provisions on dispute settlement, labor, the environment, customs administration, among other matters.

FTAs establish a framework for liberalizing trade in agricultural commodities and food products between partners within an agreed-upon time period. Achieving preferential access as much as possible to each other's market is the primary objective in negotiations, with the intent also to secure a competitive edge over third countries that sell into an FTA partner's market. Accomplishing this requires that negotiators work to reduce and eventually eliminate tariffs and quotas on most agricultural goods. Because the United States and each prospective FTA partner have some agricultural products that benefit from high levels of border protection, negotiators spend much of their time wrestling with how to transition these import-sensitive products towards free trade.

The United States also has sought to address other non-tariff barriers (particularly those dealing with food safety and animal/plant health — commonly referred to as SPS measures) on a separate, but parallel, track. Though U.S. negotiators assert that resolution of outstanding bilateral SPS disputes is not on the formal FTA negotiating agenda, press reports point toward negotiators on both sides seeking to resolve such disputes and using them as leverage to achieve other FTA negotiating objectives. Further, resolving these disputes is viewed as essential to ensure that FTA partners do not resort to using these barriers to undercut the openings created for U.S. exporters in market access talks.

MARKET ACCESS FOR IMPORT-SENSITIVE AGRICULTURAL PRODUCTS

One U.S. objective in negotiations is that bilateral free trade agreements be comprehensive (i.e., cover all products). For the more sensitive agricultural commodities, negotiators generally agree on long transition periods before tariffs and quotas are completely eliminated. Recently negotiated FTAs, though, provide for indefinite protection for a few commodities. U.S. commodities that are protected this way include sugar in four FTAs and beef in the Australia FTA. Such protection takes the form of slowly-expanding preferential tariff-rate quotas (TRQs) and the retention of prohibitive tariffs on over-quota imports in perpetuity, the use of safeguards to protect against import surges, and special mechanisms to address unique situations (see Types of Provisions in U.S. FTAs that Apply to Agricultural Trade below for an explanation of these and related terms used in this report). Details on how these and other sensitive commodities are handled differ from one FTA to another, and are laid out in lengthy and complex tariff schedules and annexes to each agreement's agriculture chapter.

For example, the Dominican Republic-Central American Free Trade Agreement (DR-CAFTA) and the FTAs with Colombia, Panama, and Peru (still awaiting congressional consideration) allow the United States to cap in perpetuity the amount of sugar that enters. In return, DR-CAFTA allows Costa Rica to indefinitely limit imports of U.S. fresh onions and fresh potatoes, and the four other Central American countries to similarly treat imports of U.S. white corn. For the United States and CAFTA countries, the in-quota amount on only these specified commodities expands from 1% to 2% each year, while the prohibitive tariff on over-quota entries never declines. Similarly, while U.S. exporters received increased access to Morocco's wheat market, Morocco will indefinitely apply a quota and a prohibitive over-quota tariff on U.S. wheat. This new way to address the sensitivity of some agricultural products is unique in the FTAs recently negotiated by the United States, and apparently does not appear in other countries' FTAs. Table 3 and table 4 list the sensitive agricultural commodities (as reflected in long transition periods or special treatment) in each current and prospective FTA, respectively. Additional information on some commodities is summarized in the FTA-by-country overviews.

Table 3. Agricultural Commodities with the Longest Transition Periods or Subject to Border Protection Indefinitely in Current U.S. Free Trade Agreements

FTA with	Commodities Sensitive to the:	
	United States	Partner Country
Canada	Dairy products, peanuts, peanut butter, cotton, sugar and sugar-containing products (SCPs)	Dairy products, poultry, chicks, eggs, turkey, margarine
Mexico	Sugar, peanuts, frozen-concentrated orange juice (FCOJ), certain winter vegetables (cucumbers, asparagus, broccoli), some processed vegetables, melons	Corn, dry beans, milk powder, sugar, dried onions, chicken leg quarters, high-fructose corn syrup, FCOJ, some processed vegetables, melons
Australia	Sugar (*excluded*), beef, dairy products, peanuts, cotton, tobacco	None
Chile	Avocados, processed artichokes, dairy products, poultry, sugar, tobacco, wine	Non-durum wheat, wheat flour, vegetable oils, poultry
Guatemala (DR-CAFTA)	Sugar, SCPs, beef	White corn, rice, chicken leg quarters, dairy products
Honduras (DR-CAFTA)	Sugar, SCPs, beef	White corn, rice, chicken leg quarters, dairy products
Israel	Butter, sour cream, dried milk, cheese and substitutes, ice cream, peanuts	Dairy products, fresh fruits and vegetables, almonds, wine
El Salvador (DR-CAFTA)	Sugar, SCPs, beef	White corn, rice, chicken leg quarters, dairy products
Singapore	None	None
Morocco	Dairy products, preserved tomato products (paste and puree), tomato sauces, dried onions, dried garlic, processed fruit products, tobacco	Wheat, beef, chicken leg quarters and wings, other poultry products, almonds, apples
Nicaragua (DR-CAFTA)	Sugar, SCPs, peanuts, beef	White corn, rice, chicken leg quarters, dairy products
Jordan	Unmanufactured tobacco and cigarettes (*excluded*)	Unmanufactured tobacco and cigarettes (*excluded*), refined corn and soybean oil
Bahrain	None	None

Source: Based on a CRS review of FTA tariff and TRQ schedules.

Table 4. Agricultural Commodities with the Longest Transition Periods or Subject to Indefinite Border Protection in Pending or Possible U.S. Free Trade Agreements

	Commodities Sensitive to the:	
	United States	Partner Country
Pending Partner		
South Korea	Dairy products	Rice (*excluded*), beef, pork, oranges, pears, apples, grapes, whey and soybeans for food use, milk powder, cheese, barley
Colombia	Dairy products, sugar, sugar-containing products (SCPs), tobacco, beef	Corn, other feed grains, rice, chicken leg quarters, whole poultry, dairy products
Costa Rica (DR-CAFTA)	Sugar, SCPs	Fresh onions, fresh potatoes, rice, chicken leg quarters
Dominican Republic (DR-CAFTA)	Sugar, SCPs, beef, dairy products, tobacco, cotton	Chicken leg quarters, rice, cheese, certain milk products
Peru	Sugar, SCPS, dairy products, avocados	Corn, rice, dairy products, chicken leg quarters
Panama	Sugar, SCPs, beef	Pork, chicken leg quarters, certain dairy products, corn, rice, refined corn oil, dried beans, frozen french fries, tomato products
Oman	None	None
Possible Partner		
Thailand	Sugar, rice	Corn, citrus, grapes, vegetables, cheese, pulses
Malaysia	None	Rice, tobacco, alcohol products

Source: Based on a CRS review of FTA tariff and TRQ schedules, Malaysian negotiators' statements to date, and USTR, *2006 National Trade Estimate Report on Foreign Trade Barriers*, March 2006.

COVERAGE OF AGRICULTURAL PRODUCTS IN FTAS

The extent to which U.S.-negotiated FTAs have led to complete free trade in agricultural products has evolved since the first two bilateral trade agreements were negotiated. The FTAs with Israel (1986) and Canada (1998) still limit bilateral trade in several import-sensitive products with the use of TRQs. However, NAFTA with Mexico (1994) will result in bilateral free trade in all agricultural products beginning in 2008.

Types of Provisions in U.S. FTAs that Apply to Agricultural Trade

Transition or **phase-out periods** refer to the time intervals used to completely remove current trade barriers (tariffs, quotas, and other forms) on agricultural products. Barriers are eliminated immediately or in stages — set at specific future points in time (e.g., 3, 5, 10, 15 years, etc.). Each stage is sometimes referred to as a "basket." Decisions by negotiators on which basket to place each product in depends on how sensitive one country perceives imports from the partner country to be to domestic producers. The longest transition periods apply to the most import-sensitive agricultural products.

Tariff elimination involves reducing a tariff to zero, by the end of the transition period agreed upon by negotiators for each agricultural product. The tariffs currently in effect are used as the starting point. For many products, tariffs are eliminated on a linear basis (i.e., equal annual reductions). For the more sensitive products, tariff reductions occur on a non-linear basis, meaning the tariff only begins to fall at the mid-point or toward the end of the transition period (i.e., backloaded).

Preferential tariff-rate quotas (TRQs) provide for duty-free access of a specified quantity of a commodity, which expands over time. Imports above this quota are subject to a tariff, which declines over time. At the end of the transition period, both the quota and tariff no longer apply, allowing for unrestricted access to the partner's market. Countries use TRQs to protect their more sensitive products. The preferential nature of a TRQ in an FTA is that one partner has a competitive advantage in selling to the other partner's market.

Safeguards protect producers of specified agricultural products against sudden import surges during the transition to free trade (e.g., as tariffs decline and/or quotas expand). Their use, automatically activated when a product's import price falls below a specified price level or when the quantity entering exceeds a specified amount, is designed to give producers additional time to adjust to increased import competition.

Rules of origin specify what is required for an agricultural product to be considered as having been produced or processed in one country, in order to be eligible for preferential treatment (e.g., in the form of a zero or declining tariff, or access under a preferential quota) when exported to the partner's market. These are designed to benefit the firms and exporters operating in the FTA participant countries, so that those of another country cannot take advantage of one partner's preferential access to the other partner's market.

Many of the more recent FTAs negotiated by both the Clinton and Bush Administrations provide for long transitions to free trade for all but a handful of agricultural commodities and food products. The three exceptions because of political sensitivities for the United States or its partners are the outright exclusions for tobacco in the Jordan FTA (2001), sugar in the Australia FTA (2005), and rice in the recently-concluded FTA with South Korea (2007).

SANITARY AND PHYTOSANITARY (SPS) ISSUES [4]

Decisions by other countries (including current and prospective FTA partners) on animal, plant, and human health and food safety issues have significantly reduced or limited U.S. agricultural sales to these markets. Though U.S. negotiators state that they do not view FTA negotiations as the forum in which to try to raise and resolve these disputes, parallel discussions on these SPS issues have affected the negotiating dynamics and the pace of concluding several recent FTAs. Also, the slow pace of movement by FTA partners in implementing side letter commitments reached on outstanding SPS issues has at times influenced the decision by the Office of the U.S. Trade Representative (USTR) on when to seek congressional approval of an FTA. Similarly, the same dynamic has influenced USTR's assessment of how to proceed to conclude an FTA or to complete the required legal steps before an FTA can enter into force. Members of Congress also have put the President and trade negotiators on notice that these issues must be dealt with before FTA talks conclude or congressional consideration proceeds. Examples of such developments are provided below in the country-by-country section.

The controversies that have surfaced reflect the growing use by countries of SPS rules, intended to ensure food safety and protect animal and plant health, as disguised trade barriers. Trade experts have observed that as quota expansion has opened up foreign markets to agricultural imports, governments face pressure to protect domestic producers from increased competition using such non-tariff measures as SPS rules. Accordingly, U.S. policymakers have concluded that resolving outstanding SPS issues is important to the U.S. agricultural sector in order for exporters to be able to take advantage of the market access openings that new FTAs can create. Exporters also have signaled that the application of SPS rules must be science-based, transparent and predictable, so that they know what applies to them when selling products to FTA partners. Their view reflects each country's rights and obligations under the WTO's 1994 SPS Agreement, which lays out rules to ensure that each country's food safety and animal and plant health laws and regulations are transparent, scientifically defensible, and fair.[5]

Even though they are not technically on the agenda, two SPS issues have concerned U.S. negotiators in recent FTA talks with several countries. One U.S. objective has been to secure an FTA partner's recognition of the U.S. meat (beef, pork, and poultry) inspection system as equivalent to its own. Panama and some Central American countries had argued that their regulatory agencies be allowed to continue their policies of accepting meat imports only from those U.S. meat processing plants that their own food inspectors had approved. U.S. exporters argued that this practice stymied sales, requiring them to comply with multiple sets of rules that were redundant to the existing U.S. meat inspection system.

Second, following the discovery of a cow with bovine spongiform encephalopathy (BSE) or mad cow disease in Washington state in December 2003, many countries imposed bans on the import of U.S. beef.[6] The United States asked the Office of International Epizootics (OIE)[7] to review its response and the validity of measures already in place to mitigate the risks of this animal disease to humans and cattle herds. Along with Canada and Mexico, the United States earlier had asked this panel to reconsider its international guidelines for determining the risk status of countries with BSE, to better reflect the adequacy of a country's safeguards. This has involved U.S. regulatory agencies presenting extensive evidence to show that U.S. beef products are safe and that U.S. human and animal safeguards are effective. In negotiating the more recent FTAs, the United States pressed prospective partners (e.g., Colombia, Malaysia, Peru, Panama, and South Korea) to recognize U.S. measures taken to address the BSE issue as conforming with internationally recognized scientific guidelines governing meat trade,[8] and to allow purchases of U.S. beef to resume. Similarly, some Members of Congress have stated that their support for the Korea FTA will depend on the measures South Korea adopts to allow U.S. beef imports to enter under the bilateral agreement reached in January 2006.[9]

To resolve these bilateral SPS issues, U.S. and FTA country negotiators have reached separate agreements or exchanged side letters that acknowledge prospective partners' acceptance of the equivalency of the U.S. meat inspection system and recognition of the steps the United States has taken to ensure the removal of beef parts that carry the risk of transmitting BSE. These frequently have stipulated the steps a partner will undertake to facilitate the entry of imports of U.S. meat products and/or commit a partner to allow U.S. beef certified as meeting specified standards to be imported by a specified date. Though these SPS side letters and agreements are not an integral part of FTA texts, the use of FTA negotiations as the opportunity to leverage resolution to longstanding SPS issues resulted in attaining market openings that would otherwise have taken much longer to achieve. For example, the United States succeeded in securing from Colombia, Peru, and Panama changes in their regulations to allow for the import of U.S. beef.

The SPS chapter in each recent FTA reaffirms each partner's rights and obligations under the WTO's 1994 SPS Agreement to also be the basis for resolving SPS issues that come up in future bilateral trade. This text establishes a SPS standing committee to facilitate consultations on, and resolve, bilateral SPS problems as they arise. The Australia FTA went further, creating a Technical Group on Animal and Plant Health Measures to work to achieve consensus on the scientific issues behind a specific SPS dispute. Unlike NAFTA with Canada and Mexico, all FTAs negotiated since 1993 prescribe that the agreement's dispute settlement process cannot be used to challenge the other partner's SPS standards.

Chapter 5

U.S. AGRICULTURAL TRADE WITH WORLD, FTA PARTNERS, AND PROSPECTIVE CANDIDATES

OVERVIEW

Over the last 25 years, two-way U.S. agricultural trade (the sum of exports and imports) has more than doubled — from $60 billion in 1981 to $136 billion in 2006. Annual trade growth averaged 5.1% during this period. However, changes in the value of the U.S. dollar and in the competitiveness of the U.S. agricultural sector, and the fallout of the Mexican and Asian financial crises in 1995 and the late 1990s, respectively, contributed at times to occasional dips in this upward trend. The increase in overall U.S. agricultural trade has been driven by two sets of factors. First, worldwide population growth, rising incomes in key export markets, and growing U.S. consumer demand for fresh fruits and vegetables account for much of this increase. Second, trade policy developments have bolstered this trend. Implementation of U.S. FTAs with Canada and Mexico, and of the multilateral 1994 Uruguay Round Agreement on Agriculture that reduced trade-distorting agricultural policies, created additional market openings for U.S. exports and imports. Also, the expansion of duty-free access under U.S. unilateral trade preference programs has boosted agricultural imports from developing countries.[10]

The share of two-way agricultural trade covered by U.S. free trade agreements increased from $329 million (just under 1%) in 1986 (under the FTA with Israel) to $54 billion (41%) in 2006 (when FTAs with 13 countries were in effect) (figure 1 and figure 2, and table 5). Growing trade with Canada and Mexico, as NAFTA significantly liberalized U.S. agricultural trade with each country, has accounted for much of the increase in two-way trade since 1989.

Over the last quarter century, total U.S. agricultural exports increased by almost two thirds — from $43 billion in 1981 to $71 billion in 2006. Export growth during this period averaged 2.5% each year, in spite of the downturns that occurred in the mid-1980s and again in the late 1990s. In 2006, agricultural exports covered by U.S. FTAs equaled $26 billion (37%) of the total, compared to $255 million (one-half of 1%) in 1986 (figure 2 and figure 3, and table 5).

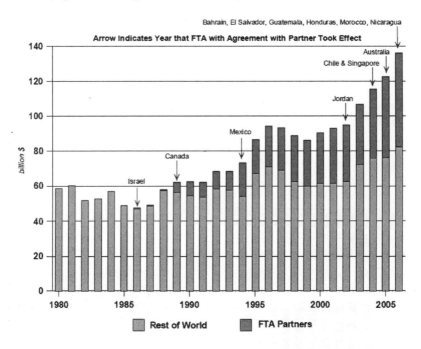

Figure 1. U.S. Agricultural Trade (Exports and Imports) Covered by Free Trade Agreements.

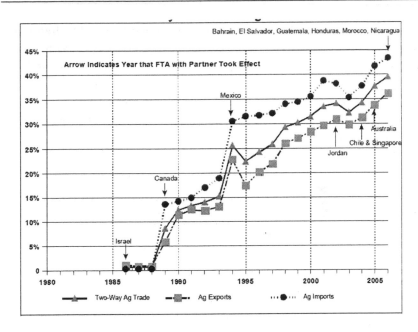

Figure 2. Share of U.S. Agricultural Trade (Total, Exports, and Imports) Covered by Free Trade Agreements.

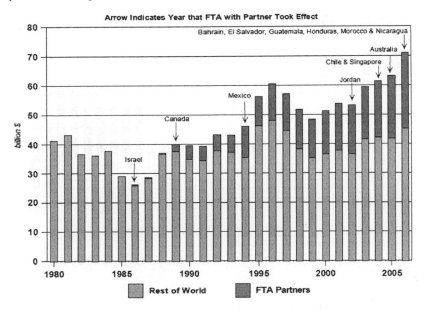

Figure 3. U.S. Agricultural Exports Covered by Free Trade Agreements.

**Table 5. U.S. Agricultural Trade with Current U.S. FTA Partners
Compared to World, Ranked by Two-Way Trade: 2006**

	Two-Way U.S. Agricultural Trade [a]	U.S. Agricultural Exports *Million Dollars*	U.S. Agricultural Imports
World	$136,326	$70,993	$65,333
Current FTA Partners			
Canada	25,363	11,930	13,433
Mexico	20,287	10,896	9,390
Australia	3,006	519	2,487
Chile	2,074	301	1,774
Guatemala (DR-CAFTA) *	1,471	548	924
Honduras (DR-CAFTA) *	617	327	290
Israel	612	414	198
El Salvador (DR-CAFTA) *	422	277	145
Singapore	382	303	79
Morocco *	374	295	80
Nicaragua (DR-CAFTA) *	358	138	220
Jordan	145	142	3
Bahrain *	16	16	0
TOTAL, Current FTA Partners	$55,128	$26,105	$29,023
Share of World	*40.4%*	*36.8%*	*44.4%*
ADDENDUM			
Subtotal, FTAs that Took Effect During 2006 [b]	$3,259	$1,600	$1,659
Share of World	*2.4%*	*2.3%*	*2.5%*

Source: Derived by CRS from trade data from USDA's Foreign Agricultural
  Service.
a. U.S. agricultural exports plus U.S. agricultural imports
b. Refers to the six countries marked by an asterisk (*) above.

Total U.S. agricultural imports have grown by nearly four times
during this period — from $17 billion in 1981 to $65 billion in 2006.
Imports have risen steadily and at a faster rate than exports. Import
growth has averaged 11.5% annually. In 2006, agricultural imports
covered by U.S. FTAs were $29 billion (44%) of the total, compared to
$74 million (one-third of 1%) in 1986 (figure 2 and figure 4, and table 5).

U.S. AGRICULTURAL TRADE WITH THE MOST RECENT AND PROSPECTIVE FTA PARTNERS

During 2006, the United States began to implement three free trade agreements with six countries (El Salvador, Guatemala, Honduras, and Nicaragua under DR-CAFTA, and Bahrain and Morocco under separate agreements). Two-way U.S. agricultural trade with these countries in 2006 totaled almost $3.3 billion (2.4% of the total). U.S. agricultural exports were valued at $1.6 billion; U.S. agricultural imports equaled $1.7 billion (see "Addendum" in table 5).

FTAs that the United States has negotiated with another seven countries could come into effect in late 2007 or 2008. This will depend on if, and when, Congress and/or a partner country's legislature approves each, and then on how quickly implementation-related issues are addressed. The FTAs concluded with Panama and

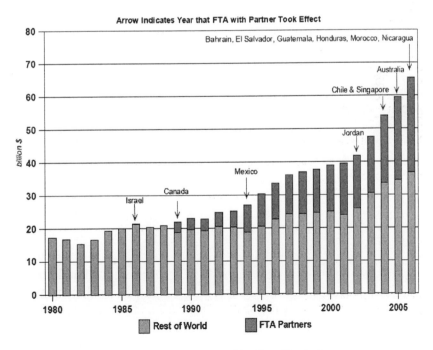

Figure 4. U.S. Agricultural Imports Covered by Free Trade Agreements.

Peru are expected to receive congressional consideration during the 1st session of the 110th Congress, with House leadership and the Bush Administration having reached deal on additional labor and environmental provisions.[11] Congress may take up the trade agreements with Colombia and South Korea if the issues of labor union violence and autos, respectively, can be addressed in a way that the Administration believes would result in additional favorable Member votes.[12] Costa Rica's legislature is following a timetable to complete consideration of DR-CAFTA by late-2007, which the U.S. Congress approved in mid-2005. If approved, DR-CAFTA provisions with Costa Rica would likely take effect in early 2008. The Dominican Republic earlier this year completed a revision of its laws and regulations to comply with DR-CAFTA's terms. In turn, USTR on March 1, 2007, announced that its provisions had gone into effect. Earlier, President Bush on September 26, 2006, signed legislation approving the FTA with Oman. This agreement may take effect, possibly later in 2007, once bilateral understandings are reached on implementation matters.

In 2006, two-way agricultural trade with these seven countries totaled $8.9 billion (6.6% of the total) (table 6). Two-way agricultural trade with South Korea and Colombia alone accounted for 60% of U.S. agricultural trade with these seven countries. U.S. commodity and food exports to these seven nations equaled $5.1 billion; agricultural imports were valued at $3.8 billion.

The United States also had been negotiating FTAs with two other countries —Thailand and Malaysia — but did not conclude these talks before the April 1, 2007 deadline for them to be considered under current TPA rules. Two-way U.S. agricultural trade with these two countries in 2006 totaled almost $3.3 billion (2.4% of the total). Agricultural exports were valued at $1.1 billion; commodity and food imports totaled $2.2 billion (table 6).

Table 6. U.S. Agricultural Trade with Prospective U.S. FTA Partners Compared to World, Ranked by Two-Way Trade: 2006

	Two-Way U.S. Agricultural Trade [a]	U.S. Agricultural Exports	U.S. Agricultural Imports
	Million Dollars		
World	$136,326	$70,993	$65,333
Countries with FTAs Not Yet in Effect, Signed, or Concluded			
South Korea	3,068	2,851	217
Colombia	2,348	868	1,480
Costa Rica (DR-CAFTA)	1,483	320	1,163
Dominican Republic (DR-CAFTA)	957	629	328
Peru	811	209	602
Panama	265	209	56
Oman	14	13	1
Subtotal	$8,946	$5,099	$3,847
Share of World	6.6%	7.2%	5.9%
Possible FTA Partners - Negotiations Underway or Suspended			
Thailand	2,038	703	1,334
Malaysia	1,248	415	832
Subtotal	$3,285	$1,118	$2,167
Share of World	2.4%	1.6%	3.3%
All Prospective FTA Partners			
TOTAL	$12,231	$6,217	$6,014
Share of World	9.0%	8.8%	9.2%

Source: Derived by CRS from trade data from USDA's Foreign Agricultural Service.

[a] U.S. agricultural exports plus U.S. agricultural imports.

Chapter 6

POTENTIAL IMPACTS OF RECENT AND PROSPECTIVE U.S. FTAS ON U.S. AGRICULTURAL TRADE

Two-way agricultural trade with the 12 countries with which the United States has approved FTAs since 2004 and with Colombia and Peru whose FTAs await congressional consideration could be an estimated 1.6% to 2.0% higher than would occur without these trade agreements.[13]

U.S. agricultural exports would be higher, largely because of the market openings created as most FTA partners' high agricultural tariffs and most other border protections are largely eliminated over time. U.S. agricultural imports would also rise, primarily from Australia and Chile, as U.S. tariffs on farm products of export interest to these countries and quotas on U.S. sensitive agricultural commodities (except sugar) are phased out completely.

CHANGE IN U.S. AGRICULTURAL EXPORTS

Trade liberalization provisions in five FTAs (covering 10 countries) could result in increases in U.S. agricultural exports of an estimated $1.1 billion (U.S. International Trade Commission (USITC) estimate) to $3.3 billion (American Farm Bureau Federation (AFBF) estimate) (table 7). The USITC estimate is 2.0% above the 2005 level for U.S. agricultural exports. The AFBF estimate is 2.7% above USDA's agricultural export baseline for 2015.[14] The wide range in estimates reflects the different methodologies used to project increases in U.S. agricultural exports as a result of the FTAs with Australia, Morocco, the six countries covered by DR-CAFTA, Peru, and Colombia (see Appendix A for an explanation). Also, both organizations project that such exports would be higher under FTAs with four other countries, but a direct comparison cannot be made. The USITC projects that exports to Chile and Singapore together would be $136 million higher. The AFBF estimates that U.S. farm product sales to Bahrain, Oman, and Panama could be $490 million higher (see "Addendum" in table 7).

Table 7. Comparison of Estimates of Change in U.S. Agricultural Trade Under Recent U.S. FTAs

	U.S. Exports		U.S. Imports *	
	U.S. International Trade Commission (USITC)	American Farm Bureau Federation (AFBF)	U.S. International Trade Commission (USITC)	American Farm Bureau Federation (AFBF)
	million US $			
Australia	+ 187.1	+ 165.0	+ 1,097.2	+ 370.0 [a] [b]
Morocco	+ 254.0	+ 259.1	+ 25.0	+ 25.0
DR-CAFTA [c]	+ 328.4	+ 1,521.3	+ 52.1	+ 80.5 [d]
Peru	+ 185.2 [e]	+ 705.8	+ 42.6	+ 6.4 [d]
Colombia	+ 170.0	+ 692.9	+ 223.0	+ 32.4 [d]
Subtotal, 10 Countries	+ $1,124.7	+ $3,344.1	+ $1,439.9	+ $514.3 [f]
Chile	+ 45.6 [a]	— -	+ 543.0 [a]	— -
Singapore	+ 90.2 [a]	— -	+ 58.8 [a]	— -
Subtotal, 2 Countries	+ $135.8		+ $601.8	
TOTAL CHANGE	+ $1,260.5		+ $2,041.7	
ADDENDUM				
Bahrain	g	+ 75.0 [a]	g	— -
Oman	g	+ 225.0	g	— -
Panama	h	+ 190.0	h	h

Notes: (1) The main difference between the USITC and AFBF estimates lies in the timing of when the agricultural provisions of each FTA are fully implemented. The USITC assumes these provisions are implemented immediately, and does not take into account the impact of various macroeconomic and sectoral changes that occur in the transition to free trade. The Farm Bureau develops all but one of its estimates for the last year of the FTA's transition period, incorporating projections of population and economic growth in the interim. (2) USITC estimates shown are derived by CRS from the details of USITC's modeling results published in each report. (3) Final analyses of the agricultural trade impacts of the Panama and Korea FTAs will be released by the USITC and AFBF later in 2007.

Sources: This CRS-derived table is based on AFBF analyses of FTAs with Australia, Bahrain, Colombia, DR-CAFTA, Morocco, and Peru; USITC reports analyzing the economy-wide and sectoral effects of these five FTAs plus those with Chile and Singapore, and an AFBF release on the Panama FTA, March 8, 2007.

* Before accounting for trade diversion (see text and footnote #16)

a. Mid point of estimated range.

b. AFBF raises the prospect that U.S. imports may be lower, ranging from $120 to $220 million on the view that Australia may not fill all of its new preferential beef quota.

c. Covers Costa Rica, Dominican Republic, El Salvador, Guatemala, Honduras, and Nicaragua.

d. Estimated value only of increased sugar imports.

e. Based on assumption that U.S. trade preference program with other Andean countries (Bolivia, Ecuador, and Colombia) expires.

f. Import estimate is not complete in coverage, because the AFBF did not include imports of agricultural commodities other than sugar in analyzing the outlook for U.S. agricultural imports under FTAs with DR-CAFTA, Peru, and Colombia. Estimates for Australia and Morocco cover all commodities.

g. USITC analyses did not consider prospects for U.S. agricultural trade under these two FTAs, likely because current trade levels are too low to be analyzed.

h. USITC's analysis of the Panama FTA is expected to be released by mid-September 2007.

CHANGE IN U.S. AGRICULTURAL IMPORTS

The USITC projects U.S. agricultural imports under the same five FTAs could increase by $1.4 billion (table 7).[15] However, the impact of trade diversion as trade flows shift from elsewhere in the world to these FTA partners lowers overall U.S. agricultural imports as a result of these agreements to about $700 million.[16] As a result, USITC's import projection (adjusted for trade diversion) could be 1.4% higher than would be the case otherwise.[17] Most of this increase would reflect additional imports from Australia, which has gained access to the U.S. market under expanding U.S. preferential TRQs for sensitive agricultural commodities (beef and dairy products). If the USITC analyses for the Chile and Singapore FTAs are added to the picture, U.S. agricultural imports could be another $600 million higher (but when adjusted for trade diversion, only $300 million more).

Australia and Chile would account for most of the increase in agricultural imports under the FTAs analyzed by the USITC. Agricultural imports from most of the other FTA partners (classified to be developing countries) have benefitted for some time from low or zero duty access under U.S. unilateral trade preference programs (Generalized System of Preferences (GSP); Andean Trade Preference; and the Caribbean Basin Initiative). As a result, the small increases shown for them in table 7 largely reflect the benefits they would receive with the additional export access gained into the U.S. market under expanding preferential TRQs for commodities that the United States has protected with quotas for some time.

Chapter 7

AGRICULTURE IN CURRENT U.S. FTAS

Of the 10 U.S. FTAs now in effect, only three have operated for more than 10 years (those with Israel, Canada and Mexico). Except for the Jordan FTA, six trade agreements have taken effect since 2004 (table 1). One-third of total two-way U.S. agricultural trade is accounted for by Canada and Mexico, largely because of the market openings created by NAFTA many years ago and both countries' proximity to the U.S. market. The rate of growth in bilateral agricultural trade with Canada and Mexico, but not with Israel, has been higher compared to the rate of increase in U.S. agricultural trade with the rest of the world during the time period that each agreement has been in effect.

Because six FTAs are relatively new (i.e., with implementation periods of three years or less), it is difficult to determine whether the growth in two-way trade is attributable solely to liberalizing trade provisions. A portion of the increase is also due to growing populations, per capita income growth, and changing diets. Also, U.S. consumers' growing demand for fruits and vegetables would likely have been met in part by imports from these partners, even without these FTAs. The more significant market access provisions gained for U.S. exporters will take time to take effect, with the long transition periods negotiated for sensitive commodities. A more detailed analysis would be required to correlate changes in commodity trade flows to specific tariff and quota provisions in these FTAs.

Agriculture as covered by each of the current FTAs is examined below in the order each country ranks in its bilateral agricultural trade with the United States (as shown in table 5). The next section surveys agriculture as covered by FTAs with prospective partner countries.

CANADA [18]

Canada is the leading agricultural trading partner of the United States, and accounted for almost 19% of two-way U.S. agricultural trade in 2006. Since the Canada-U.S. Trade Agreement (CUSTA) took effect in 1989, bilateral trade in agricultural and food products has increased more than six times (from an average $4 billion in 1986-1988, to $25.4 billion in 2006). For comparison, during this same period, U.S. two-way agricultural trade with the rest of the world slightly more than doubled.

U.S. agricultural exports to Canada increased almost seven times (from an average $1.8 billion in 1986-88 to $11.9 billion in 2006). Imports from Canada rose six times (from an average $2.2 billion in 1986-88 to $13.4 billion in 2006). In 2006, the main U.S. exports to Canada in terms of value were: vegetables — fresh, processed, frozen and dried ($1,732 million), fresh fruit ($1,122 million), breakfast cereals and baked goods ($709 million), food preparations ($495 million), beef and veal ($424 million), fruit juices ($406 million), pet food ($393 million), pork ($365 million), cocoa ($317 million), coffee ($274 million), and confectionery products ($186 million). In 2006, main U.S. imports from Canada were live cattle ($1,032 million), bakery products and snacks ($966 million), beef and veal ($923 million), pork ($889 million), fresh vegetables — primarily greenhouse tomatoes, peppers, and cucumbers ($724 million), chocolate ($690 million), frozen vegetables ($664 million), live hogs ($579 million), rapeseed oil ($424 million), confectionery products ($380 million), wheat ($304 million), food preparations ($278 million), beer ($275 million), and cheese mixes and doughs ($232 million).

Under the CUSTA's agricultural provisions (incorporated into NAFTA in 1994), almost all agricultural products have traded freely between both countries since 1998. Exceptions are those commodities that each country still subjects to tariff-rate quotas (TRQs). Canada uses TRQs to limit imports from the United States of its import-sensitive commodities (dairy products, margarine, poultry, turkey, and eggs).[19] The United States uses TRQs to restrict imports of Canadian dairy products, peanuts, peanut butter, cotton, sugar and certain sugar-containing products (SCPs). Both countries also retain the option under CUSTA to apply temporary safeguards on bilateral trade in selected fruits, vegetables, and flowers through year-end 2007. Since mid-2003, the discovery of BSE on both sides of the border has significantly affected bilateral trade in live cattle and beef products.[20]

MEXICO [21]

Mexico is the second largest agricultural trading partner of the United States, and accounted for almost 15% of two-way agricultural trade in 2006. Since NAFTA went into effect in 1994, two-way bilateral trade in agricultural and food products has more than tripled (from an average $6 billion in 1991-1993, to $20.3 billion in 2006). For comparison, during this same period, U.S. two-way agricultural trade with the rest of the world nearly doubled.

U.S. agricultural exports to Mexico rose by more than three times (from an average $3.5 billion in 1991-93, to $10.9 billion in 2006). In 2006, sales of corn ($1,472 million), soybeans ($906 million), beef and veal ($778 million), food preparations ($483 million), wheat ($418 million), cotton ($412 million), beef variety meats ($388 million), grain sorghum ($323 million), pork ($309 million), soybean meal ($255 million), and decidious fresh fruit ($245 million) accounted for more than one-half of U.S. agricultural exports to Mexico.

Agricultural imports from Mexico have almost quadrupled (from an average $2.5 billion just before NAFTA took effect, to $9.4 billion in 2006). Purchases of fresh vegetables, primarily tomatoes, chili and peppers, cucumbers, squash and onions ($2,573 million); beer ($1,600 million); fresh fruit, primarily avocados, melons, grapes, limes, mangoes, and strawberries ($1,149 million); live cattle ($524 million); confectionery products ($385 million); sugar ($320 million); and baked goods and snacks ($312 million) accounted for almost three-quarters of U.S. agricultural imports from Mexico.

Under NAFTA, tariffs and quotas on most traded agricultural products were eliminated in 2003. However, the United States and Mexico still impose border protection on a few products subject to a 15-year transition period to free trade. All such protection will end on

December 31, 2007. U.S. agricultural products that then will be eligible to freely enter the Mexican market will be: corn, dry beans, milk powder, sugar, dried onions, chicken leg quarters, and high-fructose corn syrup (HFCS); and under specified tariff lines, processed vegetables, frozen concentrated orange juice (FCOJ), and melons. Products imported into the United States from Mexico that then will be allowed to enter freely will be FCOJ, peanuts, and sugar; and under specified tariff lines cucumbers, asparagus, broccoli, melons, and processed vegetables.

All other agricultural products now enter each other's market freely, except for those that at times have become embroiled in trade disputes. Most of the bilateral disputes that have arisen since 1993 — when tariffs and quotas were eliminated for those agricultural commodities that fell in the 10-year staging category — have affected several U.S. agricultural commodities exported to Mexico (rice, beef, pork, apples, soy oil, and HFCS). At the same time, Mexican farmers and some Mexican commodity groups began pressuring the Mexican government to renegotiate certain NAFTA provisions. Calls for renegotiating NAFTA, particularly those provisions that apply to Mexico's most sensitive agricultural commodities (dry beans and corn), were an election issue in Mexico's 2006 presidential race. Though top Mexican officials under the previous presidential administration stated that reopening NAFTA was not possible and would not occur, current President Calderon continues to face heavy public pressure to revisit this position. Separately, sugar that enters from Mexico is the main sensitive product for the United States. The fact that sugar imports from Mexico will be unrestricted beginning in 2008 is already affecting the dynamics of the debate on the future U.S. sugar program as Congress considers the 2007 farm bill.[22]

CENTRAL AMERICAN COUNTRIES AND DOMINICAN REPUBLIC [23]

In the Dominican Republic - Central American Free Trade Agreement (DR-CAFTA) approved by Congress in mid-2005 after heated debate, the United States and six countries (Costa Rica, the Dominican Republic, El Salvador, Guatemala, Honduras, and Nicaragua) agreed to phase out tariffs and quotas on all but four agricultural commodities and food products immediately or under one of six phaseout periods ranging up to 20 years. Trade in four very sensitive commodities — fresh potatoes and fresh onions imported by Costa Rica, white corn imported by the other four Central American countries, and sugar entering the U.S. market — are treated uniquely in the agreement. At the end of specified periods, the quota amount set for these four commodities will continue to increase by about 1% to 2% each year in perpetuity. In other words, a quota, though rising, will always limit imports of these four commodities. The tariff on above-quota entries, though, will not decline, but stay at current high levels to protect producers. Because of its sensitivity, DR-CAFTA also commits all parties to consult and review the implementation and operation of the provisions on trade in chicken about mid-way in the long transition period to free trade.

The six countries covered by DR-CAFTA accounted for $5.3 billion, or almost 4% of two-way U.S. agricultural trade, in 2006. U.S. agricultural exports in 2006 to the six countries totaled just over $2.2 billion, which represented just over 3% of U.S. worldwide sales that year. The six countries combined represented the eighth largest export market for U.S. agricultural products. Leading U.S. exports were: corn ($443 million), wheat ($313 million), soybean meal ($246 million), rice ($175 million), tobacco ($98 million), and cotton ($86 million). The Dominican Republic was the largest of the six markets — with $629 million in sales (28% of U.S. agricultural exports to the region), followed by Guatemala ($548 million with a 25% share).

The DR-CAFTA grants immediate duty-free status to more than one-half of the U.S. farm products now exported to the six countries, according to the USTR. Such treatment applies to high-quality U.S. beef cuts, cotton, wheat, soybeans, certain fruits and vegetables, processed food products, and wine destined for the five Central American countries. Central American tariffs and quotas on most other agricultural products (pork, beef, poultry, rice, other fruits and vegetables, yellow corn, and other processed products) are being phased out over a 15-year period. Longer transition periods apply to imports from the United States of rough/milled rice and chicken leg quarters (18 years) and dairy products (20 years).

U.S. exports of corn, cotton, soybeans, and wheat to the Dominican Republic benefit also from immediate duty-free treatment. Dominican Republic tariffs and quotas on most other U.S. agricultural products (beef, pork, and selected dairy and poultry products) are being eliminated over 15 years. However, 20-year transitions will cushion the impact of the entry of U.S. chicken leg quarters, rice, and certain dairy products (cheese and milk products).

Prior to DR-CAFTA, almost all agricultural imports from the six countries already entered the U.S. market duty free. The agreement made such treatment permanent. The most significant change is that DR-CAFTA grants additional market access in the form of country-specific preferential quotas to imports from the region of U.S. import-sensitive agricultural products (sugar, sugar-containing products, beef, peanuts, dairy products, tobacco, and cotton). These quotas will be in addition to (i.e., not carved out of) the existing agricultural TRQs established by the United States under current WTO commitments, which the six countries in varying degrees historically have used to export to the U.S. market.

Drawing much attention during congressional debate were the agreement's sugar provisions which allow additional sugar from the region to enter the U.S. market. Members, particularly during a Senate Finance Committee hearing, questioned how the agreement's "sugar compensation mechanism" would work. This provision allows the United States to compensate the six countries for sugar they would not be able to ship under DR-CAFTA's preferential sugar quotas if the entry of such additional sugar is expected to undermine USDA's ability to administer the U.S. sugar price support program. This unique mechanism in U.S. FTAs (which applies only to sugar imported under DR-CAFTA and the FTAs with Colombia, Panama, and Peru) is structured to be activated and exercised at the sole discretion of the U.S. government. Though not spelled out in detail, officials have mentioned that if used, compensation could include donating surplus commodities in USDA inventories or making cash payments as compensation to sugar exporters in the six countries.

To assuage these Members' concerns, the Bush Administration pledged, prior to Senate passage, to take steps only through FY2008 to ensure that all sugar imports, including those under DR-CAFTA, do not exceed a "trigger" that could undermine USDA's ability to manage the domestic sugar program. Sugar producers and processors responded that USDA's pledge did not address their long-term concerns about the viability of the U.S. sugar program. Fearing that DR-CAFTA's sugar provisions would set a precedent for the inclusion of sugar in FTAs being negotiated with several other sugar exporting countries, the industry continued last-minute, but unsuccessful, efforts in the House to defeat the agreement.[24]

Agricultural imports in 2006 from these six countries equaled $3.0 billion, or almost 5% of all U.S. farm and food imports. Combined, these countries ranked as the fourth leading source of U.S. agricultural imports in that year. U.S. purchases of bananas ($638 million), unroasted coffee ($630 million), pineapple ($408 million), raw cane sugar ($281 million), and melons/watermelons ($180 million) led the list. Of the six, Costa Rica was the largest supplier of food products — with $1.16 billion in sales (38% of U.S. agricultural imports from the region), followed by Guatemala ($924 million, with a 30% share).

During 2006, the United States moved on a rolling basis to implement the DR-CAFTA with four countries (El Salvador, Honduras, Nicaragua, and Guatemala) once USTR determined that each had made "sufficient progress" in completing its commitments under the agreement. Provisions with the Dominican Republic took effect on March 1, 2007. Costa Rica may be added as an FTA partner by early 2008, if a public referendum approves, and its legislature ratifies, the agreement.

AUSTRALIA [25]

Efforts by Australia's negotiators to secure additional access for beef, dairy products, and sugar in the U.S. market proved to be among the most contentious issues just before the Australia-U.S. FTA was concluded in February 2004. U.S. negotiators succeeded in excluding sugar from the agreement, an objective that the U.S. sugar industry had sought, and in immediately eliminating Australia's tariffs on all imports of U.S. agricultural products. While Australia sought immediate and substantial openings for its beef and dairy products, the FTA provides for limited but growing access under quotas to the U.S. market over long transition periods. Quotas and high tariff protection on some dairy product imports will continue in place indefinitely. Negotiators also agreed to create a new mechanism to facilitate scientific cooperation between both countries to resolve bilateral sanitary and phytosanitary (animal and plant health) issues. Available analyses indicate that

CHILE [27]

On January 1, 2004, the U.S.-Chile FTA began to phase out tariffs on a substantial portion of agricultural products traded between both countries within four years (2007). However, Chile and the United States adopted up to a 12-year transition period before all import-sensitive products are free to enter from the other country. Interim protection for such products will include the use of TRQs and agricultural safeguards. The special safeguards are price-based, and will be implemented automatically using listed trigger prices. Prior to this FTA, Chile's tariff on most agricultural products was 6%. By comparison, the U.S. average tariff equivalent on agricultural imports from Chile was less than 1.5%.

Chile agreed to grant duty-free status to more than 75% of U.S. agricultural products immediately or within four years. Such treatment applies to pork and products, beef and products, soybeans and soybean meal, durum wheat, feed grains, potatoes, and processed food products (i.e., french fries, pasta, distilled spirits and breakfast cereals). Chile's tariffs and quotas on all other products are being phased out in three stages over 8, 10, or 12 years. Chile will eliminate its price bands[28] on a non-linear basis in three stages on imports of non-durum wheat, wheat flour, and vegetable oils from the United States by year 12 (2015).[29] U.S. products subject to Chile's safeguards include certain meat products; broken, brown, and partially-milled rice; rice flour; and certain wheat products. The USITC anticipates that the FTA could provide opportunities for U.S. soybean sales in off-season months and for wheat sales after the eighth year.

In 2006, likely due in part to this FTA being in effect for three years, the value of U.S. agricultural exports to Chile ($301 million) was 2-1/2 times higher than the annual average of $118 million in the three-year period (2001-2003) before the FTA took effect. Leading products shipped were corn ($48 million), wheat ($38 million), soybean meal ($36 million), corn gluten meal ($32 million), planting seeds ($16 million), almonds ($12 million), food preparations ($11 million), and animal feeds ($8 million). Chile's rank as a market for U.S. agriculture has risen from 52nd (2003) to 28th (2006).

The United States agreed to grant duty-free status to a large share of Chile's agricultural products immediately or within four years. Preferential TRQs will apply to imports from Chile of beef, poultry, cheese, milk powder, butter, condensed milk, other dairy products, sugar, tobacco, avocados, and processed artichokes. Non-linear tariff reductions will apply to imports of fluid milk and those dairy products subject to a TRQ, avocados, and wine, among other products. Chilean products covered by the U.S. safeguards include specified vegetables and fruits, various canned fruits, frozen concentrated orange juice, tomato products, and avocados. The USITC expects the U.S. dairy and "other crops" sectors will face some increased competition, and that imports of avocados and prepared/preserved fruit from Chile will increase.

Largely due to the FTA, agricultural imports from Chile rose by more than one-half in recent years (from an average $1.1 billion in 2001-02, to $1.8 billion in 2006). Leading agricultural purchases were fresh grapes ($718 million), wine ($167 million), planting seeds ($131 million), apples ($76 million), blueberries ($68 million), apple juice ($54 million), avocados ($52 million), frozen raspberries ($30 million), preserved artichokes ($20 million), dried grapes ($17 million), fresh oranges ($14 million), and frozen strawberries ($13 million). In 2006, Chile was the 9th leading supplier of U.S. agricultural imports, up from 12th in 2003.

In an example of a U.S. success in addressing a technical non-trade barrier, Chile agreed to recognize U.S. beef grading programs. This will allow for the sale of U.S. beef and pork products with the USDA prime and choice labels in Chile. One SPS issue reportedly held up the agreement's signing — Chile's acceptance of the U.S. meat inspection system as equivalent to its own — a provision that the FTA did not include. Several senators signaled to USTR that failure to reach an agreement on this issue before the FTA was signed could result in the loss of some support for the agreement. In turn, Chile quickly moved to formally accept the U.S. inspection system as providing equivalent health and food safety protection. The signing followed on June 6, 2003. Separately, in a side letter, both countries agreed to have their regulatory agencies conduct technical and scientific work to achieve mutual beneficial access for poultry products.

ISRAEL

Duty-free treatment of non-agricultural trade under the U.S.-Israel FTA took full effect on January 1, 1995. However, both countries had a decade earlier agreed that each could maintain import restrictions (i.e., quotas and fees) for agricultural policy purposes, but could no longer apply tariffs. Because of this latitude, special agricultural provisions still govern a portion of bilateral agricultural trade.

Though tariffs on agricultural products were significantly reduced from 1985 to 1994, Israel during this period took advantage of the above exception to protect its sensitive agricultural products by maintaining levies and fees on many of them, and placing quotas and import bans on others. Differences over how to interpret the scope of import restrictions and tariff concessions led both countries in 1996 to sign an "Agreement on Trade in Agricultural Products" (ATAP). This laid out a comprehensive schedule for a gradual and steady liberalization in market access for trade in these products through December 31, 2001. Under the ATAP, Israel offered lower preferential tariffs (at least 10% below its MFN rates) on some U.S. agricultural products, established duty-free TRQs for almost 100 U.S. products, and allowed unlimited duty-free entry for many other U.S. products. Under this 1996 Agreement, the United States established preferential duty-free and expanding TRQs for imports from Israel of butter and sour cream, dried milk, cheese and substitutes, peanuts, and ice cream. The ATAP was extended twice through year-end 2003, while both sides negotiated a new agreement to continue this liberalization process. This culminated in the "2004 Agricultural Agreement" — effective through year-end 2008, which provides improved access for select U.S. agricultural products (e.g., wine, almonds, and certain cheeses) to the Israeli market. The 2004 Agreement increases over time the duty-free amounts of the above five product categories allowed to enter under the U.S. TRQs created for Israel.

About 90% of the value of U.S. agricultural exports enters Israel on a duty-free and quota-free basis under its WTO, FTA, and 2004 Agreement commitments. Remaining exports (primarily consumer-oriented food products) face a complex TRQ system and high tariffs, according to USTR. U.S. products facing such restrictions include dairy products, fresh fruits and vegetables, almonds, wine, and certain processed foods. If trade barriers on these products were eliminated, industry sources estimate sales of these products could increase by $60 to $105 million.[30]

In 2006, U.S. agricultural exports to Israel totaled $414 million — down almost one quarter from the decade-earlier export level ($537 million in 1997). The decline in U.S. sales in recent years has been matched by the growth in agricultural exports from Switzerland and the European Union (which also have FTAs with Israel but are geographically closer) and Argentina. In 2006, Israel ranked 21st as a market for U.S. agriculture. Leading U.S. commodities sold were corn ($120 million), soybeans ($68 million), wheat ($29 million), almonds ($26 million), soybean meal ($15 million), and pet food ($13 million). U.S. agricultural imports from Israel in 2006 were $198 million — twice the 1997 level. More than one-half of the imports from Israel are accounted for by baked goods and snacks ($24 million), spices ($19 million), vegetable seeds ($14 million), vegetable saps for medical purposes ($14 million), peppers ($9 million), ornamental foliage ($6 million), tomato paste and preserved tomato products ($6 million), cocoa preparations ($6 million), and flower bulbs ($5 million).

SINGAPORE

With Singapore one of the leading U.S. trading partners in Southeast Asia and the regional headquarters for many U.S. corporations, the Clinton Administration initiated FTA negotiations with this city state in late 2000 as part of its policy to enhance U.S. access to the "Big Emerging Markets."[31] With two-way agricultural trade a small share of total bilateral trade, and with Singapore a net importer of agricultural products but with a large food processing sector, this FTA's agricultural provisions were easy to negotiate. This was in large part due to the fact that Singapore's applied tariffs on most imports of agricultural commodities and food products were already zero before this agreement took effect on January 1, 2004.

In 2006, U.S. agricultural exports to Singapore totaled $303 million, compared to $79 million in agricultural imports. Reflecting a diverse composition of products exported, food preparations ($25 million), preserved reptile skins ($22 million), nonfat dry milk ($13 million), broiler meat ($12 million), oranges ($10 million), frozen potato french fries ($10 million), and grapes ($9 million) accounted for one-third of sales. Top agricultural imports from Singapore were cocoa butter/oil ($24 million), baked goods ($11 million), niger seed — an oilseed ($3 million), tea preparations ($3 million), stearic acids and salts ($3 million), and wool grease ($3 million).

Under the FTA, Singapore eliminated its remaining tariffs immediately — on beer and samsu (a regional liquor). Singapore harmonized its high excise tax on imported and domestic distilled spirits in 2005; this tax still applies to imports of wine and tobacco products. Though a contentious issue in the negotiations, Singapore finally agreed to allow imports of chewing gum (previously forbidden to be consumed) "with therapeutic value for sale and supply" to be sold in pharmacies, subject to laws and regulations that govern health products.

The United States will eliminate duties on all agricultural imports from Singapore immediately or in stages over 4, 8, or 10 years, depending on product sensitivity. Preferential TRQs are in place until 2013 on imports from Singapore of sensitive agricultural products (beef, fluid milk products, cheese, milk powder, butter, other dairy products, peanuts, sugar, cotton, and tobacco), but only if produced in Singapore. Because it is a major shipping hub in southeast Asia, the rules of origin developed for U.S. sensitive agricultural products are intended to prohibit duty-free treatment of any food products transhipped from neighboring agricultural producing countries in that region via Singapore to the U.S. market.

FTAs usually provide for a process to accelerate the pace of removing trade barriers if both countries agree. An example of this was Singapore's request in March 2006 on behalf of its nut snack manufacturers for an increase in its 2007 preferential peanut quota — from 1.3 MT to 200 MT. Singapore argued that these firms could then offer a wider range of peanut snacks, processed from U.S.-origin peanuts, that could be shipped in commercially meaningful quantities that would benefit not just U.S. peanut growers but also U.S. consumers. Several U.S. peanut grower groups and processors contacted USTR to express their opposition to this proposal, arguing that since Singapore is not a peanut producing or exporting country, peanuts would be sourced from other origins to take advantage of this quota increase. Concerned that this would set "a terrible precedent," U.S. peanut growers, shellers, and manufacturers argued that FTAs "should not set up new cottage industries that grow at the expense of our domestic peanut industry." In May 2007, USTR announced the FTA's peanut quota will not be expanded, noting that Singapore's exporters could utilize the existing U.S. peanut TRQ under its WTO commitment to expand sales to the U.S. market.[32]

MOROCCO[33]

Agriculture was difficult for Morocco to negotiate in its FTA with the United States, because this sector accounts for 15-20% of the country's gross domestic product and 40-45% of its labor force. Small-scale farmers dominate this sector, with many producing wheat. For this reason, reaching agreement on the terms of access in the Moroccan market for U.S. wheat was the most sensitive agricultural issue that negotiators faced.

In 2006, Morocco ranked 29th as a market for U.S. agricultural exports, which totaled $295 million. Sales of five commodities — corn ($126 million), soybeans ($70 million), durum wheat ($33 million), soybean meal ($16 million), and crude soybean oil ($18 million) — accounted for 89% of the total. Six products accounted for more than three quarters of the $80 million in agricultural imports from Morocco — processed olives ($29 million), olive oil ($15 million), fresh mandarin oranges ($8 million), a thickener derived from locust beans and guar seeds ($6 million), agar-agar — used as a thickening agent in food and as a base for bacterial culture media ($4 million), and tomato powder ($3 million).

Under the FTA, which took effect on January 1, 2006, Morocco agreed to reduce tariffs and expand preferential quotas on all agricultural imports from the United States immediately or under one of 9 phase-out periods ranging up to 25 years. The longest transition will apply to imports of U.S. chicken leg quarters and wings. Morocco will offer access under expanding TRQs to its market for U.S. high quality beef for its restaurant/hotel sector, standard quality beef, whole birds —chickens and turkeys, chicken leg quarters and wings, other frozen chicken products, durum wheat, common bread wheat, wheat products, sugar and sugar-containing products, almonds, and apples. Morocco also secured the right to implement a licensing system for imports of U.S. high-quality beef destined for the hotel/restaurant sector. A "preference clause" provides U.S. exporters with "better market access" for U.S. wheat, beef, poultry, corn, soybeans, and corn/soybean products in case Morocco negotiates more favorable terms in the future with other countries. This is intended to enable U.S. exporters compete with the European Union and other countries that might broaden or initiate improved trade ties with Morocco.

Because of the sensitivity of the wheat sector, complex provisions detail the terms of U.S. access to the Moroccan market. These differentiate between durum wheat and common bread wheat. While the in-quota tariff on durum imports will be reduced to zero from the current 75% over 10 years, the preferential in-quota tariff on common wheat imports will decline using a formula that applies whenever Morocco's current 135% applied MFN rate is lowered. This preferential tariff will not be available to U.S. exporters during June and July (and possibly August for common wheat) of any year, unless Morocco imports either type of wheat from another country, in which case U.S. wheat will then receive the preferential rate. Over-quota tariffs for both wheat types will remain at current high levels indefinitely, unless Morocco negotiates a reduction with another supplier. If this occurs, U.S. exporters will automatically benefit from this wheat tariff reduction. The preferential quota for common wheat will be based on the level of Moroccan wheat output — a smaller quota if production is 3 million MT or more; a larger quota if output is less than 2.1 million MT. While the durum wheat quota will expand slowly indefinitely, the common wheat quota will increase during the first 10 years and then be capped indefinitely beginning in 2015. In other words, while U.S. wheat will benefit from much improved access to the Moroccan market, a quota and a prohibitive over-quota tariff will always apply. Also, Morocco secured the right to operate a wheat auction system for in-quota imports of U.S. wheat.

The United States similarly agreed to eliminate tariffs and offer preferential quota access to all agricultural imports from Morocco under seven phase-out periods: immediately, or 5, 8, 10, 12, 15, or 18 years. The longest transition (18 years) is reserved for six designated processed fruit products. The United States established preferential TRQs for beef, dairy products (including fluid milk products, cheese, milk powder, butter), sugar and sugar-containing products (SCPs), peanuts, tobacco, cotton, tomato products (including tomato paste and puree), tomato sauces, dried onions, and dried garlic. Imports of sugar and SCPs are subject to a "trade surplus" calculation, meaning that Morocco can sell the lower of: its preferential quota or the amount by which all of its exports of specified sugar products exceed imports of similar products.[34]

The USITC estimates that full implementation would result in an increase in U.S. exports to Morocco of primarily grains and processed food and tobacco products. The small increase in imports would primarily take the form of processed food products.

JORDAN [35]

The U.S.-Jordan FTA went into effect in December 2001. Though bilateral trade was modest at that time, this agreement was one of several U.S. strategic initiatives to assist the Jordanian economy and develop closer ties with an Arab country in the Middle East.

This FTA eliminates tariffs on almost all bilateral trade by the 10th year (2010). One exception is that trade in unmanufactured tobacco and cigarettes is exempt from tariff elimination. Pertinent to the more significant agricultural products traded, Jordan phased out its 5% tariff on imports of U.S. rice, corn, and unrefined vegetable oils at year-end 2004. Jordan's 30% tariff on imports of U.S. refined corn and soybean oil will be eliminated by 2010. Wheat will continue to enter free as before. Also, Jordan did not create TRQs for any U.S. agricultural product. A USITC analysis concluded that this FTA likely will lead to negligible increases in total U.S. exports of rice, corn, and vegetable oil. It noted that to be competitive in the Jordanian market, U.S. exporters had relied on USDA credit programs to sell these commodities. In return, Jordan secured 10-year preferential TRQs to export several agricultural commodities that meet the FTA's rules of origin: dairy products, sugar and sugar-containing products, peanuts/peanut butter, and cotton.

In 2006, U.S. agricultural exports to Jordan ($142 million) were 39% above the average ($103 million) recorded in the three-year period (1999-2001) before the FTA took effect. Leading exports were corn ($64 million), non-durum wheat ($18 million), rice ($16 million), almonds ($10 million), corn oil ($7 million), and soybean meal ($5 million), which accounted for 84% of the total. Wheat historically had been the leading U.S. export, supported by long-term concessional credits extended under PL 480 Title I — a U.S. food aid program. Agricultural imports from Jordan are very small, but have quadrupled from an average $731,000 in 1999-2001 to $3 million in 2006. Principal imports were processed chickpeas ($805,000), sauces and condiments ($535,000), baked goods ($231,100), and spices ($233,000).

BAHRAIN [36]

Bahrain, a small island state with limited land suitable for agriculture, is a significant net agricultural importer. U.S. farm and food exports ($15 million in 2006) were quite diverse, led by sales of protein concentrates ($1.4 million), chicken meat ($1.3 million), beef ($1.3 million), and frozen potato french fries ($1.1 million). Prior to the FTA, Bahrain imposed a 5% tariff on semi-processed and consumer-ready food products. In the early 2000s, tariffs were eliminated on many other foods, including fresh fruit and vegetables. Congress approved the FTA in December 2005, and the agreement took effect on August 1, 2006. Bahrain agreed to provide immediate duty-free access for U.S. agricultural exports on 98% of its agricultural tariff lines, and to phase out tariffs on all other products within 10 years. In recognition that the United States since 2001 has recorded zero agricultural imports from Bahrain, all of Bahrain's current exports of farm products to the U.S. received immediate duty-free access.

Chapter 8

AGRICULTURE IN PENDING FTAS

The 110th Congress in coming months may consider the FTAs concluded with South Korea, Colombia, Panama, and Peru under current trade promotion authority, or fast track rules, that limit debate, prohibit amendments to implementing legislation, and require a simple up or down vote. The FTA with South Korea would be the most commercially significant for U.S. agriculture since NAFTA took effect with Mexico in 1994. Though already approved by the United States, the Oman FTA will not take effect until outstanding issues are resolved.

With the early May 2007 agreement between House leadership and the Bush Administration on a new trade framework that adds labor, environmental, and other provisions to these four pending FTAs, Congress is expected this fall to consider the agreements with Panama and Peru. However, the timing for congressional consideration of the other two is uncertain. Prospects for the Colombia FTA are clouded by concerns over labor union violence in that country. Also, while some Members of Congress want to renegotiate the auto provisions in the Korea FTA, the Korean Government is reluctant to incorporate the new trade framework's labor provisions or reopen the issue of auto access.

Agriculture as covered in each pending FTAs is examined below in the order each country ranks in its bilateral agricultural trade with the United States (as shown in table 6).

SOUTH KOREA [37]

On April 1, 2007, U.S. negotiators concluded an FTA with their South Korean counterparts some 20 minutes before the expiration of the deadline set in the TPA statute. This required the President to notify Congress of the Administration's intent to sign this agreement by this date to be considered under TPA procedures. Compromises on the final package that provide for much improved access for all U.S. agricultural products (except for rice) to the Korean market were reached in the final hours. The agreement was signed on June 30, 2007. However, numerous Members of Congress have signaled that their support is contingent on Korea following through on its other commitments to fully reopen its market to U.S. beef (see below).

Increasing market access for U.S. agriculture to the large Korean market was the main objective for USTR's agricultural negotiators. This reflected the interests of the US agricultural sector, which eyes much potential for further export gains, particularly in sales of higher-value food products to an expanding middle class. In 2005, South Korea was the world's 8th leading agricultural importing country. At the same time, its agricultural sector is highly protected, reflecting the political influence of its farmers and the urban population's deep ties to its rural roots. South Korea's average applied agricultural tariff (2005) was 42%.[38] Average applied tariffs are highest for vegetable products (over 100%); average tariffs for other broad agricultural product categories range from 8% to 23%. Tariffs on pistachios and walnuts are 30%, on pork between 22.5% and 25%, on poultry products from 18% to 27%, and on fruit juices from 30% to 54%. Also, Korea extensively uses TRQs to limit imports of rice, oranges, various dairy products, potatoes, onions, grains, and other agricultural products. For example, the over-quota tariff on soybeans is 487% (increased to 649% in 2006, if the import volume rose above a specified trigger level). The prohibitive over-quota tariff on barley ranges from 300% to 513%, on oranges is 50%, on corn for feed is 328%, and on milk powder is 176%. Though rice imports under a restrictive quota are subject to a 5% tariff, over-quota entries are prohibited (a unique concession that South Korea received during the Uruguay Round agricultural negotiations).

In 2006, U.S. sales accounted for 25% of South Korea's $12.5 billion agricultural import market. However, the U.S. share of South

Korea's import market has declined over the last decade, as China, Australia, and Brazil have expanded sales. In 2006, South Korea was the 6th largest market for U.S. agriculture, with export sales totaling almost $2.9 billion. Leading commodities sold were corn ($718 million), whole cattle hides ($259 million), pork ($204 million), non-durum wheat ($188 million), soybeans ($113 million), cotton ($103 million), and hay ($95 million). U.S. agricultural imports from South Korea were much smaller in comparison ($217 million), primarily accounted for by purchases of food preparations ($44 million), pasta wheat products — likely ramen noodles ($31 million), fresh pears ($21 million), non-alcoholic beverages ($21 million), baked goods and pastries ($18 million), and rice wine ($5 million).

Under the FTA's agricultural provisions, South Korea immediately would grant duty-free status to almost two-thirds of current U.S. agricultural exports ($1.9 billion). USTR notes that most of the remaining agricultural tariffs and quotas will be phased out within 10 years after taking effect. In particular, Korea agreed to phase out tariffs, quotas, and safeguards on all but seven agricultural products under 12 phase-out periods ranging up to 23 years. Seasonal provisions would apply to U.S. sales of oranges, table grapes, and potatoes for chipping.[39] Tariffs on many fruits, vegetables and food products would be eliminated in two or five years. Tariffs on the more sensitive commodities (e.g., beef, in-season potatoes for chipping, pears, apples, in-shell walnuts, and in-season grapes) would be phased out in15 to 20 years. Tariff-rate quotas (TRQs) also with long phase-out periods (10 to 18 years) would apply to such other sensitive products as cheeses, butter, dairy-based infant foods, barley, whey for food use, animal feed supplements and hay, corn starch, and ginseng. USDA notes that these TRQs lock in access that South Korea could have easily changed under its multilateral trade commitments. Slowly-expanding quotas would apply in perpetuity on imports from the United States of skim and whole milk powders, evaporated milk, in-season oranges, potatoes for table use, honey, and identity-preserved soybeans for food use. Unique to this FTA, South Korea secured the right to specify the state entities and trade associations that would administer each TRQ under either an auction or licensing system. Safeguards (e.g., applying special add-on tariffs in case of import surges) would be triggered if imports from the United States of some of these and other agricultural products exceed specified levels.

metric tons (MT) and sales of another 13,000 MT were in the pipeline.[44]

On May 22, 2007, the OIE voted to accept the recommendation that the United States is a "controlled risk" country for the spread of BSE. USDA immediately requested that South Korea amend its import requirements for U.S. beef within a specified time frame to reflect this risk determination and to reopen its market "to the full spectrum of U.S. cattle and beef products." Korea responded that its animal health regulatory agency would follow an 8-step process to carry out its risk assessment of the U.S. beef sector, but did not lay out a timetable. With a few steps already completed, bilateral talks on an expanded agreement governing U.S. beef sales could begin by late summer. The United States will advocate including exports of bone-in beef in addition to boneless beef from cattle less than 30 months old (currently allowed), and expanding the agreement's scope to apply to all U.S. beef from cattle irrespective of age, as long as BSE-risk materials are removed during processing. While several members of Congress and much of the U.S. beef industry have responded positively to Korea's clearance of beef shipments, their support of the FTA is conditioned upon Korea fully opening up its market before Congress takes up the agreement.[45] Accordingly, they will be closely monitoring Korea's multi-step process in completing its assessment and the progress of bilateral talks on a broader beef access agreement.

COLOMBIA [46]

Though U.S. agriculture would gain from significant additional market access to Colombia under the concluded FTA, concerns expressed by some Members of Congress over the violence directed at labor union officials in that country has affected congressional consideration of this trade agreement.

Ranked as the 14th largest market worldwide for U.S. agriculture in 2006, Colombia is the second largest market for U.S. farm products in Latin America after Mexico. U.S. sales accounted for more than one third of Colombia's agricultural and food imports, recording sales of $868 million in 2006. Leading exports were corn ($366 million), wheat ($89 million), cotton ($67 million), soybeans ($65 million), and soybean meal ($62 million). Agricultural imports from Colombia totaled almost $1.5 billion, led by unroasted coffee ($595 million), fresh roses ($206 million), bananas ($143 million), fresh bouquet flowers ($111 million), fresh carnations ($67 million), fresh chrysanthemums ($63 million), and raw cane sugar ($45 million).

The United States and Colombia formally signed the FTA on November 22, 2006. Though difficult agricultural issues took almost another six months to resolve after negotiations were concluded in late February 2006, the signing ceremony was not scheduled until Colombia took steps to fulfill a separate commitment to allow by no later than October 31, 2006, the entry of U.S. beef imports (see below).

The FTA with Colombia eliminates tariffs and quotas on all agricultural products traded bilaterally (except for sugar) and establishes long transition periods for the more sensitive commodities. The United States secured immediate duty-free access to Colombia for more than one-half of its current exports by value. This will apply to high quality beef, bacon, cotton, wheat, soybeans, soybean meal; apples, pears, peaches, and cherries; and frozen french fries and cookies, among others.

Also, Colombia agreed to immediately eliminate price bands[47] for some 150 products — a mechanism that adds fees onto existing tariffs that fluctuate depending upon world prices. This effectively results in a higher level of border protection than would usually be the case. Its tariffs on most of its other farm and food products will be eliminated immediately or phased out in periods ranging from 3 to 15 years. For its most sensitive commodities (including those subject to price bands), Colombia will expand quotas and eliminate over-quota tariffs — 12 years for corn and other feed grains, 15 years for dairy products, 18 years for chicken leg quarters, and 19 years for rice. Both countries also commit to consult and review the implementation and operation of provisions on trade in chicken about midway through the long transition period.

Though U.S.-Colombian negotiators announced the completion of FTA talks in late February 2006, remaining differences over two agricultural market access issues were not resolved until July 8, 2006. However, a separate SPS issue dealing with the terms of access under which U.S. beef and beef products would be allowed to enter Colombia was not resolved until August 21, 2006, when the Colombian government in an exchange of letters committed to permit such imports of cattle over 30 months old, by no later than October 31, 2006.[48] On August 24, President Bush notified Congress of his intent to enter into an FTA with Colombia. Once Colombia issued regulations to fulfill its beef import pledge on October 27, the White House agreed on November 22, 2006 as a date for the FTA's formal signing. Though an FTA does not technically address the substance of SPS issues, this timeline illustrates how the U. S. negotiators exercised leverage to achieve a desired outcome for the domestic beef sector. This likely reflected the Administration's recognition that such efforts were essential to gain support from an agricultural group that may be vital to secure the agreement's approval by Congress.

Almost all of Colombia's agricultural exports to the United States would continue to benefit from current duty free access under the Andean Trade Preferences Act. The additional sugar allowed entry into the U.S. market would be treated uniquely. The United States agreed to triple Colombia's access to the U.S. sugar market — from its historic 2.3% share of the U.S. raw cane sugar TRQ (25,273 MT) — by an additional 50,000 MT of sugar and specified sugar products in the first year. This new preferential quota would increase by 750 MT annually, while the high U.S. tariff on over-quota sugar entries would remain in place in perpetuity. The Colombia FTA also includes a sugar compensation provision similar to that found in DR-CAFTA. Also, U.S. preferential TRQs were established for imports from Colombia of beef, specified dairy products, and tobacco.

The USITC projects that the gains for U.S. agriculture will accrue primarily to the rice, corn, wheat, and soybean sectors. It also projects that sales of beef, pork, and processed foods will increase. It says that the increased access for Colombian sugar and sugar-containing products to the U.S. market likely will have only a minor effect on U.S. imports and production. Cut flower imports from Colombia could increase if permanent duty free access stimulates investment in the country's flower sector and diverts trade away from other flower-exporting countries in South America.[49]

PERU [50]

The FTA concluded with Peru in December 2005 eliminates tariffs and quotas on all agricultural products traded bilaterally (except for sugar) and establishes long transition periods for its more sensitive commodities. Currently, Peru's tariffs on agricultural imports range up to 25%. Under the FTA, the United States secures immediate duty-free access for almost 90% of its current farm exports to Peru (e.g., high quality beef, cotton, wheat, soybeans, soybean meal, and crude soybean oil; such fruits and vegetables as apples, pears, peaches, and cherries; almonds; and such processed foods as frozen french fries, cookies, and snack foods). Peru also agreed to immediately eliminate price bands[51] on about 40 products, such as corn, rice and dairy products, to be replaced in part by TRQs with long transition periods. The variable tariffs on these commodities vary with world prices and can rise as high as Peru's WTO bound rate of 68%. Peru's tariffs on other agricultural products will be phased out under seven transition periods ranging from 2 to 17 years. For the more sensitive commodities, Peru will expand quotas and reduce over-quota tariffs as follows: 10 years on beef variety meats, yellow corn, and refined soybean oil; 12 years on standard quality beef; 15 years on butter, yogurt, processed dairy products, and yogurt; and 17 years on chicken leg quarters, rice, cheese, and milk powder. Both countries also commit to consult and review the implementation and operation of provisions on trade in chicken about midway through the long transition period.

Since almost all of Peru's agricultural exports to the United States currently enter duty-free under the Andean Trade Preference Program, the FTA would give Peruvian exporters more access to the U.S. market for four commodities that the United States protects using TRQs. Preferential TRQs will allow expanding access under quotas for imports from Peru of processed dairy products for 15 years, and of cheese and condensed/evaporated milk for 17 years. Sugar will be treated uniquely. The agreement allows Peru to export sugar and sugar-containing products under a preferential quota (9,000 MT in the first year, growing by 180 MT annually in perpetuity) but only if Peru shows a sugar trade surplus. This is expected to occur infrequently, because Peru varies between being a net sugar exporter and importer from year to year. A separate annual 2,000 MT quota was also created for organic sugar. The high U.S. over-quota tariff on sugar imports will remain in place indefinitely. The additional access represents a 20% increase to the minimum 43,175 MT of sugar that Peru now ships to the U.S. market under its historic 3.9% share of the U.S. raw cane sugar TRQ. A sugar compensation provision similar to that found in DR-CAFTA is also included.

In 2006, Peru ranked 37th as a market for U.S. agriculture exports. The U.S. held a 16% share of Peru's agricultural import market, with export sales totaling $209 million. Leading commodities shipped were corn ($44 million), cotton ($43 million), wheat ($19 million), soybean meal ($12 million), and soybean oil ($10 million). U.S. agricultural imports from Peru were $602 million, led by fresh asparagus ($130 million), unroasted coffee ($120 million), raw cane sugar ($39 million), processed artichokes ($34 million), processed asparagus ($33 million), paprika ($31 million), and mangos ($24 million).

In reviewing the Peru FTA's draft implementing bill that the Administration had forwarded to Congress for review, the Senate Finance Committee on July 27, 2006, adopted a non-binding amendment to its statement of administrative action.[52] This action reflected Members' frustration with the lack of movement by Peru in opening up its market to all U.S. beef without any age restrictions. The amendment required the executive branch to ensure that Peru has taken necessary steps to meet its obligations on SPS measures and technical barriers to trade by the time the FTA takes effect. Peru had earlier committed (but not fully followed through) in two side letter exchanges to allow imports of U.S. beef, beef products, and chicken by March 1, 2006, and not having done so, to open up its market to certain beef products and offal by April 12[53][3] and to all U.S. beef imports no later than May 31. The Finance Committee amendment added pressure on Peru to allow imports of beef from U.S. cattle older than 30 months that do not contain specified BSE risk material. Peru in a third exchange of letters agreed to allow such imports to enter by October 25, 2006, a decision likely prompted in part by its government's objective to have the U.S. Congress consider this FTA during the 2006 post-election lame duck session.[54] In late June 2007, Peru's legislature approved the text of the new trade framework as worked out between the Bush Administration and House leadership. This is expected to lead to a decision soon by the White

House on when to send this FTA to Congress for a vote — likely before adjournment this fall.

The USITC projects that most of the gains for U.S. agriculture from this FTA will accrue to the wheat sector. Sales of corn, rice, cotton, beef, dairy products and processed foods also are expected to rise. Its noted that the permanent tariff-free treatment accorded asparagus may lead to additional investment in Peru by U.S. growers-suppliers and processors, result in U.S. imports of fresh asparagus occurring year round, and make Peru a more competitive supplier in the U.S. market relative to other asparagus producing countries.[55]

PANAMA [56]

On December 19, 2006, after almost a year's hiatus, U.S. and Panamanian negotiators reached agreement on a comprehensive FTA that includes market access provisions of export interest to U.S. agriculture. Though separate from this trade agreement, both governments on the next day also signed an agreement detailing how SPS measures and technical standards will be applied to bilateral agricultural trade. With these near-simultaneous developments, both sides resolved outstanding differences over Panama's earlier unwillingness to accept the U.S. meat inspection system[57] and achieved a balance in bilateral market access for sensitive agricultural products (sugar for the United States; rice and corn for Panama). Congressional consideration of this agreement is expected later in 2007, now that the labor and environmental provisions of the U.S. new trade framework have been formally incorporated into the FTA text, which both countries signed on June 28, 2007.

The United States runs a strong positive agricultural trade balance with Panama, which ranked 36th as an overseas market for U.S. agriculture in 2006. U.S. agricultural exports totaled $206 million, led by corn ($34 million), soybean meal ($28 million), wheat ($20 million), various food preparations ($11 million), and rice ($10 million). U.S. agricultural imports from Panama were $56 million. Top imports were raw cane sugar ($18 million), unroasted coffee ($11 million), fresh melons ($7 million), fresh pineapple ($2 million), and pumpkins and yams ($3 million).

Under this FTA, almost two-thirds of present U.S. farm exports to Panama would receive immediate duty-free treatment, according to USDA. This will apply to sales of high quality beef, mechanically de-boned chicken, frozen whole turkeys and turkey breast, pork variety meats, whey, soybeans and soybean meal, crude vegetable oils, cotton, wheat, barley, most fresh fruits (including apples, pears, and cherries), almonds, walnuts, many processed food products (including soups and chocolate confectionary), distilled spirits, wine, and pet food. Panama also agreed to establish preferential TRQs for U.S. pork, chicken leg quarters, specified dairy products, corn, rice, refined corn oil, dried beans, frozen french fries, fresh potatoes, and tomato paste. The longest transition period (20 years) will apply to rice, Panama's most sensitive agricultural commodity. However, it agreed to increase tariff-free access for U.S. rice if needed to cover a shortfall in domestic output. Tariffs on imports of most other U.S. agricultural products would be phased out within 15 years.

Almost all of Panama's agricultural exports to the United States already enter duty free under the Caribbean Basin Initiative and Generalized System of Preference trade preference programs. Of U.S. commodities subject to quota protection, much attention focused on the additional access granted to sugar from Panama. The United States agreed to create three preferential TRQs for sugar and sugar-containing products . The largest duty-free TRQ (6,000 MT for raw sugar) will expand by 60 MT (1%) annually for 10 years and then be capped at 6,600 MT indefinitely; all sugar product over-quota tariffs will remain indefinitely at current high levels. These quotas in the aggregate represent most of the sugar surplus that Panama traditionally has available to export each year. This FTA also includes a sugar compensation provision similar to that found in DR-CAFTA. Other U.S. preferential TRQs were established for cheeses, condensed and evaporated milk, and ice cream, to be phased out completely in 15 to 17 years.[58]

In the separate SPS agreement, Panama agreed to accept the U.S. meat and poultry inspection system "as equivalent to its own." This means that all facilities that USDA certifies as meeting food safety standards to produce for the U.S. market are eligible to export meat products, and do not need further inspection by Panama. The SPS agreement also commits Panama to provide access for all U.S. beef and poultry, and related products, on the basis of accepted international standards. It also streamlines import documentation requirements for U.S. processed foods and affirms Panama's recognition of the U.S. beef grading system. USDA notes that this agreement eliminates "long-standing regulatory barriers faced by a variety of U.S. products" in Panama's market.[59]

OMAN [60]

With very limited arable land, Oman is a net agricultural importer. The U.S. market share of the country's agricultural imports is small — almost 2% in 2004, with most of its food needs met by the United Arab Emirates, Japan, and the United Kingdom. In 2006, U.S. food exports to Oman totaled $13 million, led by sales of corn ($3.1 million), flavored sugar used as beverage bases ($2.6 million), thickeners derived from locust beans ($914,000), non-far dry milk ($892,000), and mixed seasonings ($611,000). Most of the $1 million in food imports from Oman was accounted for by baked goods and snacks.

Oman's average applied tariff on agricultural products in 2005 was just over 6%. Processed food products face a 5% tariff, but basic commodities (i.e., grains, fresh fruit and vegetables, beef and poultry, powdered milk) are exempt. Pork and products, alcoholic beverages, and dried lemons are assessed a 100% tariff.[61]

The U.S.-Oman FTA concluded in October 2006 commits Oman to immediately allow duty-free entry for U.S. products entering under 87% of its agricultural tariff lines. Oman will phase out duties on most other agricultural products over five years, and by year 10 for those subject to the highest tariff. The United States will provide immediate duty-free access for 100% of Oman's current exports of agricultural products, which totaled only $2 million in 2005. Preferential TRQs phased out over 10 years will allow duty free access to the U.S. market for beef and specified dairy products, among other sensitive commodities, but only if produced in Oman. The President signed legislation to implement this FTA on September 26, 2006. Bilateral consultations on matters still outstanding have yet to conclude, before this agreement can take effect.

Chapter 9

AGRICULTURE IN FTAS WITH
POTENTIAL PARTNERS

FTA negotiations with two other countries — Thailand and Malaysia — did not conclude before the end March 2007 deadline that would have allowed for congressional consideration under TPA authority. Talks with Malaysia will continue, with many issues (including some on agriculture) reportedly still outstanding. At present, negotiations with Thailand likely will not resume, even after late 2007 elections are held for a new government, because of significant Thai public opposition. If negotiations on either of these FTAs do conclude, Congress may consider such an agreement under new TPA provisions (if and when approved). But the Bush Administration also could decide to press ahead for congressional consideration. This would depend on whether political advisors gauge that the level of opposition to either FTA likely will not be overwhelming enough to result in congressional rejection.[62] Agriculture as handled in talks to date is examined below in the order each country ranks in its bilateral agricultural trade with the United States (as shown in table 6).

THAILAND [63]

U.S. agriculture views Thailand as a promising market if FTA negotiations result in a significant reduction in its high tariffs on agricultural imports and provide increased access for its many quota-protected products. U.S. agricultural exports by one estimate could increase by an additional $800 million if Thai trade barriers are reduced or eliminated and the country's economy recovers to pre-1997 financial crisis levels.[64] Thailand similarly intends to pursue increased access for its fruit, vegetables, and sugar in the U.S. market, but its negotiators at the same time face strong opposition from Thai farmers and resistance within the bureaucracy to opening up the country's market. After six negotiating rounds had taken place, Thailand suspended the talks in February 2006 because of the country's political crisis. The government set up after the September 2006 military coup initially appeared to be committed to pursuing an FTA and having its legislature consider any possible deal, but there are no plans at present to resume negotiations.

In 2006, Thailand was the 16th largest market for U.S. agriculture, with export sales totaling $703 million. Top commodities sold were soybeans ($122 million) cotton ($147 million), wheat ($81 million), animal feeds ($36 million), whole cattle hides ($31 million), and food preparations ($29 million). U.S. agricultural imports from Thailand were just over $1.3 billion, led by purchases of natural rubber ($409 million), processed fruit - with more than one-half pineapple ($198 million), rice ($187 million), food preparations ($$86 million), and non-alcoholic beverages ($42 million).

Thailand's average applied MFN tariff rate on agricultural imports is 24%, but tariffs on consumer-ready food products range from 30% to 50%, with some as high as 90% (e.g., coffee). High tariffs are imposed on imports of meat, fresh fruits such as citrus and table grapes, vegetables, fresh cheese, and pulses, even though according to USTR these are products that have very little domestic production. TRQs also serve to protect corn, among other commodities, in a policy that USTR characterizes as designed to protect domestic producers. In the FTA talks, U.S. negotiators reportedly sought to have Thailand manage its agricultural TRQs more transparently, and to address such issues as the burdensome requirements involved in securing import permits and the high fees required to be paid to obtain import licenses. Ironing out food safety and health issues reportedly received much discussion in the talks, with USTR seeking to address complaints that Thai SPS standards on some agricultural products "often appear to be applied arbitrarily and without prior notification."[65]

Thailand was the 4th largest sugar exporter in the world in 2005/06 , and holds a historic 1.3% share of the minimum U.S. raw cane sugar TRQ. If negotiations resume, Thailand will continue to seek increased access for its sugar and rice in the U.S. market.

MALAYSIA [66]

Besides seeking improved access to its food market, one U.S. objective in negotiating an FTA with Malaysia is to eliminate its regulatory and licensing non-tariff barriers to agricultural imports. These apply to imports of all meat, processed meat, poultry, egg, egg products, rice and products, and unmanufactured tobacco, among others. U.S. negotiators also will likely seek to streamline and make more transparent the process for U.S. exporters to receive *halal* certification for livestock and poultry products, and processed foods.[67]

Though Malaysia is the world's leading producer and exporter of palm oil, it is a net food importer. In 2005, the U.S. share of its consumer food market was 7%. Malaysia's simple average applied tariff on agricultural imports was 3.2% that year. Many agricultural commodities (meat, grains, oilseeds, and animal feed) have zero or low applied tariffs, but some horticultural products (dried fruit, mixed nuts, and kiwi) and processed foods (frozen/preserved vegetables, soups, fruit juices) face applied tariffs of up to 30%. TRQs are in place for poultry, pork, preserved meat products, milk, coffee, cabbage, wheat flour, and sugar, but have no practical effect because over-quota tariffs are currently zero and quotas do not apply.[68]

In 2006, Malaysia ranked 22nd as an overseas market for U.S. agriculture. U.S. agricultural exports totaled $410 million, while agricultural imports (primarily noncompetitive commodities) equaled $829 million. Leading U.S. exports were soybeans ($50 million), fresh grapes ($40 million), non-fat dry milk ($40 million), food preparations ($31 million), tobacco ($19 million), fresh apples ($19 million), and corn gluten meal ($18 million). Top U.S. imports from Malaysia were refined palm oil ($248 million), natural rubber ($151 million), refined palm kernel oil ($132 million), cocoa butter ($91 million), and industrial fatty acids ($62 million).

In January 2007, Malaysia publicly stated its intention to exclude rice, tobacco and alcohol products in an FTA with the United States. A government corporation is the country's only authorized rice importer, and exercises broad power to regulate imports under Malaysia's licensing system. It also is charged with promoting the sale of domestic rice output.[69] One report suggests that Malaysia wants to exclude rice for national security reasons, and tobacco and alcohol for public health reasons. Sugar appears not to be an issue, because Malaysia imports much of its sugar to meet domestic demand. In the last rounds of negotiations, both sides continued to discuss their initial market access offers on agricultural products, which they first exchanged in December 2006. Some progress reportedly was made on the text of the agriculture chapter, with agreement reached on the staging periods in which to place commodities and food products for purposes of then negotiating tariff reductions. Another issue — Malaysia's plan to introduce compulsory labeling for products containing genetically modified organisms by year-end 2007 — concerns U.S. negotiators because of its potential to restrict U.S. agricultural exports.[70]

Although the end-March deadline passed for the United States to conclude an FTA which Congress could then have considered under TPA rules that allow no amendments and only an up or down vote, both sides agreed to continue negotiations. At the sixth formal session held in mid-April 2007, Malaysia reportedly still sought to exclude rice but signaled it might agree to including tobacco in the FTA. However, one earlier report suggested that Malaysia's trade minister does not view rice as a contentious issue, pointing out that U.S. rice is different from the variety produced in Malaysia and also more expensive. He also indicated that tobacco could be included if imported only as an unprocessed commodity.[71]

Chapter 10

CONCLUDING OBSERVATIONS

Most of the recently negotiated FTAs will open to varying extents markets for U.S. agriculture in countries with high levels of border protection for their agricultural sectors. In particular, U.S. agricultural trade with those FTA partners that have benefitted from a long period of preferential access to the United States will quickly take on a more reciprocal character. As their trade barriers to imports of U.S. agricultural products are reduced, U.S. agriculture and agribusiness exporters, where they have a competitive edge over other countries in these markets, will be able to take advantage of these sales opportunities. At the same time, some U.S. commodity sectors will face competition from increased imports under these FTAs. The degree of such competition will be mitigated by negotiated long transition periods and by likely continued growth in U.S. demand for such products due to population growth. Looking ahead, as transition periods to free trade for the more sensitive agricultural products near their end, disputes are likely to arise. This has been the case under NAFTA for several agricultural products, as free trade loomed, or actually took effect, and led affected producers in Canada, Mexico, and the United States to seek relief from the impacts of increased imports.

Reflecting this outlook, most U.S. agricultural commodity groups, agribusiness and food manufacturing firms have supported these recently negotiated FTAs, looking to benefit from preferential and guaranteed increased access to these markets. The largest general farm organization — the American Farm Bureau Federation —has supported all of these

FTAs but did not expect the agreement with Australia to result in an overall net gain for U.S. agriculture. The Farm Bureau views these trade agreements as the best way to reduce foreign barriers and expand export opportunities or face the prospect of reduced domestic farm production. The two leading national cattlemen trade organizations have held similar, but at times, differing positions on the beef provisions in certain FTAs, in large part due to the different geographic base of their membership.

Opposition to FTAs has come from those U.S. commodity groups concerned with the impact of increased competition from foreign producers. The extent of opposition has varied by agreement, depending upon the sensitivity of increased imports from each FTA partner, the length of transition periods, and whether special provisions are included to provide some measure of long-term protection. Such groups represent producers and processors of sugar, cotton (initially with respect to DR-CAFTA), and certain processed vegetables. Another general farm organization — the National Farmers Union — opposed DR-CAFTA. It views other trade agreements as forcing U.S. producers to compete unequally with farmers from FTA partner countries, who have a cost of production advantage because they are not required to meet the same labor and environmental standards.

Taking into account this mix of support and opposition to FTAs found in the agricultural and related food sectors, U.S. trade negotiators have sought to craft bilateral trade agreements keeping in mind the political realities involved in securing final congressional approval. It reflects a USTR FTA negotiating strategy to limit U.S. trade concessions on U.S. sensitive agricultural commodities in order to minimize opposition in Congress on any concluded agreement.

APPENDIX A. METHODOLOGIES USED TO ESTIMATE CHANGES IN U.S. AGRICULTURAL TRADE UNDER FTAS

The projections developed to illustrate expected changes to U.S. agricultural exports and imports as these FTAs are implemented vary significantly, because of the different analytical approaches used to derive them. What is common in the simulations developed by the U.S. International Trade Commission (USITC) and the American Farm Bureau Federation (AFBF) is that they seek to present what would happen to U.S. agricultural trade under each FTA compared to a "baseline" that represents what each expects such trade would be without an agreement.[72] Their approaches, however, differ in the scope of analysis undertaken and in how each handles the timing of full implementation of an FTA's agricultural trade liberalization provisions. These differences, in turn, largely explain the difference in estimates in the change in U.S. agricultural exports and imports attributable just to these agreements (table 7). The USITC employs a multi-country and multi-commodity/services sector econometric model to quantify what the broad and sectoral impacts of FTA market access provisions would mean for the entire U.S. economy. The AFBF also uses an econometric model, but employs a narrower methodology to examine what only happens to each FTA partner's main agricultural commodity sectors as border protection is eliminated. It then quantifies the resulting demand that would be met with increased agricultural imports from the United States.

Another significant difference is that the USITC assumes all FTA provisions are fully implemented and its full effects felt immediately (i.e., in the first year that an agreement takes effect) . In other words, the U.S. economy is no different in this first year from what it is in the baseline — with the same population, resources, and other economic characteristics. By contrast, the AFBF projects the change in an FTA partner's agricultural trade with the United States at a point during, or at the end of, long transition periods. This is derived by looking at the impact of adjustments expected to occur in each country's agricultural sector (as trade liberalization takes effect over time), population growth, and assumed higher economic growth and per capita incomes associated in part because of its FTA with the United States. Because USITC analyses do not take into account that the more significant agricultural provisions in an FTA are staged in over long periods (up to 20 to 25 years), nor that income levels and population likely will grow over time, its projections probably understate the magnitude of the change in U.S. agricultural exports and imports attributable to these agreements. The Farm Bureau's estimates may overstate the magnitude of the projected higher level of U.S. agricultural exports, because of overly optimistic assumptions on the potential future U.S. market share for key agricultural commodities in some FTA partner countries

REFERENCES

[1] Under the trade promotion authority enacted in 2002, Congress authorized the President to enter into trade agreements and to have their accompanying implementing bills considered under expedited legislative procedures. The TPA statute (Title XXI of P.L. 107-210) prescribes certain obligations the President's negotiators must meet in concluding such agreements, and lays out a timetable for their consideration by Congress. The latter begins with a presidential notification to Congress of his intent to sign an agreement, followed by a number of requirements (with accompanying deadlines) to be met during this process (see "Appendix A" in CRS Report RL33743, *Trade Promotion Authority (TPA): Issues, Options, and Prospects for Renewal*, J. F. Hornbeck and William H. Cooper, for an illustrated time line). The deadline to conclude negotiations with Korea was April 1, 2007, in order to meet the statutory requirement that President Bush notify Congress at least 90 days before the last day that TPA authority was in effect (June 30, 2007).

[2] Title XXI (Trade Promotion Authority) of P.L. 107-210 (Trade Act of 2002); 19 USC 3801-3813. For a listing of TPA's detailed objectives for agricultural negotiations, see CRS Report 97-817, *Agriculture and Fast Track or Trade Promotion Authority*, by Geoffrey S. Becker and Charles E. Hanrahan, pp. 5-6.

[3] These objectives, among others, frequently were laid out in letters from the U.S. Trade Representative sent to the Speaker of the House and the President Pro Tempore of the Senate, notifying

Congress of the President's intent to initiate FTA negotiations with a specified country.

[4] For additional background on the issues covered in this section, see CRS Report RL33472, *Sanitary and Phytosanitary (SPS) Concerns in Agricultural Trade*, by Geoffrey S. Becker.

[5] For a more detailed description of this Agreement, see Ibid., pp. 11-12.

[6] For background on how the presence of BSE risk in U.S. cattle herds has affected U.S. beef exports and on the actions the U.S. government has taken to address this risk to regain overseas markets, see CRS Report RS21709, *Mad Cow Disease and U.S. Beef Trade*, by Charles E. Hanrahan and Geoffrey S. Becker. For information on the steps taken against the introduction and spread of BSE, see CRS Report RL32199, *Bovine Spongiform Encephalopathy (BSE, or 'Mad Cow Disease'): Current and Proposed Safeguards*, by Sarah A. Lister and Geoffrey S. Becker.

[7] The OIE is the international scientific body recognized by the WTO as the international reference for matters of animal disease and health. One if its responsibilities is to assess the degree to which a country's policies have addressed the risk of an animal disease being introduced to another country via trade.

[8] For a further explanation, see CRS Report RS22345, *BSE ("Mad Cow Disease"): A Brief Overview*, by Geoffrey S. Becker.

[9] Office of Senator Max Baucus, "Baucus Comments on Expected Signing of Korea Free Trade Agreement," June 29, 2007; Office of Senator Charles Grassley, statement on South Korea's acceptance of U.S. beef shipment, April 27, 2007.

[10] For more information and perspective, see CRS Report 98-253, *U.S. Agricultural Trade: Trends, Composition, Direction, and Policy*, by Charles E. Hanrahan, Beverly A. Banks, and Carol Canada; and CRS Report RS22541, *Generalized System of Preferences: Agricultural Imports*, by Renee Johnson.

[11] USTR, "Statement from Ambassador Susan C. Schwab on U.S. trade agenda:", May 10, 2007; Office of Speaker of the House, "Pelosi Statement on New Trade Policy Recognizing International Labor and Environmental Standards," May 10, 2007.

[12] For more on the auto issue in the FTA with Korea, see CRS Report RL33435, *The Proposed South Korea-U.S. Free Trade Agreement*

(KORUS FTA), by William H. Cooper and Mark E. Manyin, sections on "Automobiles" and "Autos and Autoparts."

[13] This estimate is based upon a CRS review of USITC reports that analyzed the impacts of seven FTAs. The AFBF, using a different methodology, arrives at a higher estimate. See Appendix A for additional perspective and a description of methodological differences. Table 7 lists the countries covered by the analysis in this section.

[14] The benchmarks used to derive the percentage change in U.S. agricultural exports as a result of these FTAs are selected to reflect the methodology applied in each set of analyses. The sum of USITC export estimates is compared to the 2005 U.S. agricultural export level. The AFBF estimates for different future years are adjusted to 2015, the last year of USDA's export baseline projections issued in February 2006, with their sum compared to that year's USDA projection.

[15] The AFBF did not project changes in U.S. agricultural imports that could be compared to USITC-simulated import levels under these FTAs. That is because AFBF projections shown in the last column in Table 7 only reflect the value of additional sugar imported from DR-CAFTA's six countries, Peru, and Colombia. However, the AFBF-projected imports under the FTAs with Australia and Morocco can be compared to those developed by the USITC for these two countries in terms of product coverage, but were developed using different methodologies as explained in Appendix A.

[16] Trade diversion occurs when one member of an FTA shifts imports of a product away from a non-partner country (even if it is a more efficient producer) to its FTA partner (even if that product is produced less efficiently there) because the removal of the tariff (and other border protection) makes it cheaper to import that product from its partner. To illustrate, the AFBF's analysis on the Australia FTA suggested that Australian cheeses will become more competitive in the U.S. market than European-origin cheeses (i.e., resulting in a shift, or diversion, in some cheese imports from France or Switzerland, to Australia). This likely would be due to the U.S. preferential tariff and quota treatment granted to Australian cheese, while U.S. imports of European cheeses would

continue to be subject to tariffs and quotas. The USITC's analysis of the Peru FTA suggests that U.S. imports of cut flowers would be diverted from Colombia to Peru, if Colombia did not receive similar trade benefits in its own FTA with the United States.

[17] The benchmark used to derive the percentage change in U.S. agricultural imports as a result of these FTAs is consistent with the methodology used by the USITC in its analyses. Here, the sum of USITC's import projections, adjusted for trade diversion, is compared to the 2005 U.S. agricultural import level.

[18] See also the ERS Briefing Room on 'Canada' at [http://www.ers.usda.gov/Briefing/ Canada/] for pertinent reports on U.S. agricultural trade with Canada and the ERS report referenced in footnote #21, *NAFTA at 13: Implementation Nears Completion*, March 2007.

[19] These import restrictions are an integral part of the supply-management programs administered for milk, eggs, poultry, chicks, and turkeys at the provincial and national levels. Other components involve production quotas and producer marketing boards that regulate and stabilize the supply and farm prices that farmers receive for these commodities.

[20] For additional background on the major U.S. agricultural trade issues with Canada (wheat, corn, and cattle and beef), see CRS Report 96-397, *Canada-U.S. Relations*, coordinated by Carl Ek.

[21] For an overview of U.S. agricultural trade with Mexico under NAFTA, see USDA, ERS, *NAFTA at 13: Implementation Nears Completion*, by Steven Zahniser, March 2007 (available at [http://www.ers.usda.gov/publications/wrs0701/wrs0701.pdf]). See also ERS Briefing Rooms on 'NAFTA' at [http://www.ers.usda.gov/Briefing/NAFTA/] and 'Mexico' at [http://www.ers.usda.gov/Briefing/Mexico/]; and chapter 5 [Agriculture] in *NAFTA Revisited: Achievements and Challenges*, by Gary C.Hufbauer and Jeffrey J. Schott, Institute for International Economics, October 2005, for additional background on U.S. agricultural trade with Mexico and issues that have arisen under NAFTA.

[22] For more on this issue, see "Sweetener Disputes with Mexico" in CRS Report RL33541, *Sugar Policy Issues*, by Remy Jurenas.

[23] See also CRS Report RL32110, *Agriculture in the U.S.-Dominican Republic-Central American Free Trade Agreement (DR-CAFTA)*, by Remy Jurenas; and CRS Report RL31870, *The Dominican Republic-Central America-United States Free Trade Agreement (CAFTA-DR)*, by J.F. Hornbeck.

[24] For background, see "Sugar in DR-CAFTA - Sugar Deal to Secure Votes" in CRS Report RL33541, *Sugar Policy Issues*, by Remy Jurenas.

[25] See also CRS Report RL32375, *The U.S.-Australia Free Trade Agreement: Provisions and Implications*, by William H. Cooper.

[26] Because U.S. beef exporters saw sales to key Asian markets plummet immediately after the December 2003 initial mad cow incident, U.S. negotiators succeeded in including an FTA provision that prohibited sales of Australian beef under its preferential quota into the U.S. market for three years (through 2007) unless U.S. beef exports to the world return to their 2003 level. This threshold has not been reached, with USDA projecting that U.S. beef and veal sales to the world in 2007 will be 585,000 MT, about one-half of the 2003 U.S. beef export level of 1,142,000 MT (USDA, FAS, *Livestock and Poultry: World Markets and Trade*, April 2007, p. 10). In 2008, Australia's preferential beef quota will be 20,000 MT.

[27] See also CRS Report RL31144, *The U.S.-Chile Free Trade Agreement: Economic and Trade Policy Issues*, by J. F. Hornbeck.

[28] This mechanism serves to insulate producers and processors from the trade impact when the world price for any commodity falls below a calculated reference price (e.g., a price target comparable to a commodity support level). The domestic sector is protected by a variable fee on the imported commodity, which when added to the lower world or a selected international reference price, raises the importer's cost to this adjusted import price. This fee can fluctuate, depending on changes in the reference price (adjusted for freight, insurance, and other factors) to equal this pre-determined minimum import price. Colombia, Peru, and some Central American countries also use price bands. As in the Chile FTA, the FTAs with these other countries convert the level of border protection that their price bands provide into a relatively high over-

quota tariff — frequently the product's bound rate —which is then reduced to zero during the transition period.

[29] For these products, the tariff will be phased out beginning in year 5, declining from 31.5% to 21% in year 8, and then falling by more than 5% each year to zero in year 12.

[30] USTR, *2006 National Trade Estimate Report on Foreign Trade Barriers*, pp. 330-331.

[31] For background, see CRS Report RL31789, *The U.S.-Singapore Free Trade Agreement*, by Dick K. Nanto.

[32] USTR, "Singapore FTA Rules of Origin Comments," as accessed at [http://www.ustr.gov /World_Regions/Southeast_Asia_Pacific/ Singapore/ Singapore_ FTA_Rules_of_Origin_ Comments/ Section_Index.html] on April 26, 2007; *Inside U.S. Trade*, "U.S. Denies Peanut, Polycarbonate Changes in Singapore FTA," May 18, 2007, p. 13.

[33] See also CRS Report RS21464, *Morocco-U.S. Free Trade Agreement*, by Raymond J. Ahearn.

[34] For additional details, see USTR Fact Sheet, "U.S.-Morocco Free Trade Agreement Agriculture Provisions," July 6, 2004, available at [http://www.ustr.gov/assets/ Document_ Library/ Fact_Sheets/2004/ asset_upload_file176_5095.pdf].

[35] USITC, *Economic Impact on the United States of a U.S.-Jordan Free Trade Agreement*, Publication 3340, September 2000, pp. 5-1, 5-2, 5-9; WTO, Committee on Regional Trade Agreements, "Free Trade Area between the United States and Jordan - Goods Aspects-Communication from the Parties," WT/REG134/3, 2 March 2004, pp. 1-2, and "Free Trade Agreement between the United States and Jordan - Questions and Replies," WT/REG134/5, 6 January 2005, p. 1. See also CRS .Report RL30652, *U.S.-Jordan Free Trade Agreement*, by Mary Jane Bolle.

[36] See also CRS Report RS21846, *U.S.-Bahrain Free Trade Agreement*, by Martin A. Weiss.

[37] See also CRS Report RL33435, *The Proposed South Korea-U.S. Free Trade Agreement (KORUS FTA)*, by William H. Cooper and Mark E. Manyin; and CRS Report RL30566, *South Korea-U.S. Economic Relations*, by Mark E. Manyin.

[38] WTO, Statistics Database, "Country Profile for Republic of Korea," as accessed at [http://stat.wto.org/CountryProfiles/

KR_e.htm] on January 22, 2007. USDA though notes that South Korea's current average tariff on U.S. agricultural products is higher, at 52%.

[39] Quotas and/or tariffs, and transition periods, would vary, depending upon the time period that a product enters Korea's market.

[40] USTR, "United States and the Republic of Korea Sign Landmark Free Trade Agreement," June 30, 2007, p. 2. A detailed description of commodity-specific market access provisions (transition periods, TRQ amounts and growth rates, and safeguards) is found in the USDA fact sheet — "U.S. - Korea Free Trade Agreement Benefits for Agriculture (available at [http://www.fas.usda.gov/info/factsheets/Korea/ Koreagenera l0607.pdf]).

[41] For information on the steps the United States has taken against the introduction and spread of BSE, see CRS Report RL32199, *Bovine Spongiform Encephalopathy (BSE, or 'Mad Cow Disease'): Current and Proposed Safeguards*, by Sarah A. Lister and Geoffrey S. Becker.

[42] Inside U.S. Trade, "Korea FTA Talks Yield No Major Breakthroughs as of March 29," March 30, 2007, p. 17.

[43] South Korean Blue House, "Address to the Nation," April 2, 2007. In early March, a committee of the World Organization for Animal Health — known as OIE by its French acronym (see footnote #7) — had made a preliminary recommendation that the United States be classified as "controlled risk" for BSE, meaning that "OIE-recommended, science-based measures are in place to effectively manage any possible risk of BSE in the [U.S.] cattle population."

[44] As of June 28, 2007; derived from USDA's Foreign Agricultural Service "Export Sales Query System" accessed at [http://www.fas.usda.gov/esrquery/]. For comparison, by late June 2003 (the last year that U.S. beef had access to South Korea's market), U.S. beef exports already totaled more than 104,000 MT, and another 42,000 MT in sales had not yet been shipped.

[45] *Office of Senator Max Baucus, "Baucus Comments on Expected Signing of Korea Free Trade Agreement," June 29, 2007; Office of Senator Charles Grassley, statement on South Korea's acceptance of U.S. beef shipment, April 27, 2007*; American Meat Institute, "AMI Hopes that Shipment of Beef that Cleared Korea is Sign of

New Cooperation on U.S. Beef Imports," April 27, 2007; Agriculture Coalition for U.S.-Korea Free Trade, "Groups Urge Congress To Pass Korea Trade Deal," July 2, 2007, accessed at [http://www.nppc.org/wm/ show.php?id=699 and c=1].

[46] See also CRS Report RS22419, *U.S.-Colombia Trade Promotion Agreement* [CTPA], by M. Angeles Villarreal. For a detailed description of its agricultural provisions, see USDA, FAS, "U.S.-CTPA Overall Agriculture Fact Sheet," December 2006 (available at [http://www.fas.usda.gov/info/ factsheets/ColombiaFTA06.pdf]).

[47] See footnote #28 for a more comprehensive explanation.

[48] For background on this issue, see the CRS reports cited in footnotes #6 and #8.

[49] USITC, *U.S.-Colombia Trade Promotion Agreement: Potential Economy-wide and Selected Sectoral Effects,* Publication 3896, December 2006, pp. 3-1 to 3-3.

[50] See also CRS Report RS22391, *U.S.-Peru Trade Promotion Agreement* [PTPA], by M. Angeles Villarreal. For a more detailed description of its agricultural provisions, see USDA, FAS, Fact Sheet on "U.S.-Peru Trade Promotion Agreement, May 2006 (available at [http://www.fas.usda.gov/ info/factsheets/ PeruTPA-May06.pdf]).

[51] See footnote #28 for a more comprehensive explanation.

[52] The TPA statute requires the President, when forwarding to Congress a bill to implement a trade agreement, to include this statement. It describes the changes the bill makes to existing law and the significant administrative actions to be taken, in order to implement U.S. obligations under the agreement.

[53] The date both countries formally signed the FTA.

[54] *Inside US Trade*, "Finance Considers Peru Draft FTA, Approves Beef Amendment," July 28, 2006; BNA, *International Trade Daily*, "Senate Finance Recommends Peru Fully Open Markets to U.S. Beef," July 28, 2006. Text of the three exchanges of letters is available at [http://www.ustr.gov/Trade_Agreements/Bilateral/ Peru_TPA/Final_ Texts/Section_Index .html]

[55] USITC, *U.S.-Peru Trade Promotion Agreement: Potential Economy-wide and Selected Sectoral Effects,* Publication 3855, June 2006, pp. 3-1 to 3-2, 3-7, 3-18 and F-11.

[56] See also CRS Report RL32540, *The U.S.-Panama Free Trade Agreement*, by J. F. Hornbeck. Pages 11-13 provide additional background on the SPS issue and the context surrounding market access for Panama's sensitive agricultural products.

[57] The FTA talks collapsed in January 2006, when Panama's Agriculture Minister resigned, stating that USTR's request that the trade agreement include a side letter accepting USDA's safety certification would lower the country's food and health standards and increase the risk of introducing animal diseases. Since then, Panama's government changed its position, and agreed to sign this separate SPS agreement.

[58] A detailed description of commodity-specific market access provisions (transition periods, TRQ amounts and growth rates, and safeguards) is found in the USDA fact sheet "U.S.-Panama Trade Promotion Agreement Benefits for Agriculture, July 2007,"available at [http://www.fas.usda.gov/info/factsheets/Panama/ Panamaoverall 0707.pdf].

[59] Ibid., p. 1.

[60] See also CRS Report RL33328, *U.S.-Oman Free Trade Agreement*, by Mary Jane Bolle.

[61] WTO, Statistics Database, "Country Profile for Oman," September 2006, as accessed at [http://stat.wto.org/CountryProfiles/OM_e.htm] on January 24, 2007; USDA, FAS, "Oman -Food and Agricultural Import Regulations and Standards - Country Report 2006," GAIN Report MU6001, July 19, 2006, pp. 4, 8.

[62] For perspective, see CRS Report RL33743, *Trade Promotion Authority (TPA): Issues, Options, and Prospects for Renewal*, by J. F. Hornbeck and William H. Cooper.

[63] See also CRS Report RL32314, *U.S.-Thailand Free Trade Agreement Negotiations*, by Raymond J. Ahearn and Wayne M. Morrison, and CRS Report RL32593, *Thailand: Background and U.S. Relations*, by Emma Chanlett-Avery.

[64] Derived from USTR, *2006 National Trade Estimate Report on Foreign Trade Barriers*, "Thailand," p. 641.

[65] Ibid., pp. 638-641.

[66] See also CRS Report RL33445, *The Proposed U.S.-Malaysia Free Trade Agreement*, by Michael F. Martin. For more information, see

USDA, FAS, 'U.S. — Malaysia Free Trade Agreement' (available at [http://www.fas.usda.gov/itp/Malaysia/us-malaysiafta. asp]).

[67] Letter to House Speaker Hastert from USTR Announcing U.S. Intent to Negotiate FTA with Malaysia, March 30, 2006, pp. 1, 3 [Executive Communication 6881]; USTR, *2006 National Trade Estimate Report on Foreign Trade Barriers*, March 31, 2006, "Malaysia," pp. 430, 432. *Halal* refers to the slaughtering and processing of these food products in accordance with Islamic practices.

[68] WTO, *Trade Policy Review - Malaysia*, December 12, 2005, pp. 36, 39, 77-78, 80; USDA, FAS, "Malaysia Exporter Guide Annual 2006," GAIN Report MY6042, October 19, 2006, pp. 14-15, 19.

[69] U.S. Department of State, "Imports of Rice at Issue in U.S. Trade Negotiations with Korea [and Malaysia]," May 2006 (available at [http://usinfo.state.gov/ei/Archive/ 2006/May/ 12-286336.html]); *The Star Online* [Kuala Lumpur], "Tobacco, Rice Excluded in FTA Negotiations with the US," by Mergawati Zulfakar, January 15, 2007.

[70] *Inside U.S. Trade*, "U.S., Malaysia to Continue Trade Talks; No Progress On Tough Issues," March 23, 2007, p. 2; BNA's *International Trade Daily*, "Malaysia to Stand Fast on Data Exclusivity, GMO Labeling in Free Trade Talks with U.S.," April 25, 2007.

[71] *Inside U.S. Trade*, "U.S. Insists Malaysian FTA Still Possible Under Fast Track," January 19, 2007; *Inside U.S. Trade*, "U.S., Malaysia Show Increased Flexibility in Sixth Round of FTA Talks," April 27, 2007, p. 2.

[72] The only common feature in both the USITC and AFBF analyses of FTA effects are estimates on projected changes in U.S. agricultural exports and imports — measures that capture part of the prospective gains and losses experienced by U.S. agriculture under these FTAs. Both sets of analyses do not convert what FTA-caused changes in agricultural trade mean for net U.S. farm income (except for the AFBF's Morocco report), U.S. farm commodity prices, or other indicators that directly measure the economic health of the U.S. agricultural sector.

INDEX

Q

R

S

T

U

V

W

Y